Confound It!

A Collection of Recollections

Shirley J Foor

FLOATING LEAF PRESS

CHARLOTTE, NORTH CAROLINA

Cover art by Adrien Foslin.
Learn more at
facebook.com/BlueJsArt
Contact him at
4416 19 Ave W, Bradenton, Florida 34209
Adrienfoslin@gmail.com

Published in the United States of America by

FLOATING LEAF PRESS

A division of
WordPlay
Maureen Ryan Griffin
6420 A-1 Rea Road, Suite 218, Charlotte, NC 28277
Phone: 704-494-9961
Email: info@wordplaynow.com
www.wordplaynow.com

Library of Congress Control Number: 2020905120
ISBN 978-1-950499-09-0

In loving appreciation for these consistent, insistent, and persistent encouragers: Rose, Laurie, Sharon, Beverly, Tomara, Patricia, Ginny, Susan Le, Cathy, Merrie Lynn, and Ruth. Divine intervention gave life to your encouraging words. This collection of recollections celebrates your faith in my storytelling.

Contents

Introduction Recollections, Not Memories 7

Preface: Is It a Memory or a Recollection? 9

Life on the Mountain Trail 12

Racing Down Deadman's Hill 14

Learning at the Seat of Contempt 19

Humility and Pride 25

The Stain of Impulse 27

The Case of the Talking Nose 31

Beauregard the Beagle Hound 36

Our Adventure in the Circle of Life 40

A Spider Broke My Heart 47

The Power of Odd 51

The Pots and the Kettle 53

You Must Leave Now! 56

The Paddlers Did Not Linger at the Lodge 62

The Tuxedo Junction 68

Surfing Backward 76

Riding the Rapids 82

Gargle? With Lidocaine? 96

Germs Are Our Friends 101

Hokey Pokey in the Tub 103

Uncle Jim and the Infuriating Hens 108

Practice, Practice, Practice............................ 113
A Dream Shattered 121
Success after 57 Years................................. 123

Homework in the Rain 129

About the Author 131

Recollections, Not Memories

Confound It! is a collection of recollections that come with a purpose. My stories recall significant events from the life of a fairly ordinary person: me. Still, the fairly ordinary events about which I write have contributed to the uniqueness of my life, the richness of its warp and woof. The purpose of sharing these recollections, as I have for years, is to prime your memory pump.

We all have memories. These are the "make nice" pieces of our mind. Our recollections, which give strength and depth to our memories, put the flesh of the senses on the bones of those memories. From my perspective, recollections remind us with sensory detail that, yes, by gosh, we engaged in that tomfoolery, we survived those experiences, we were blessed. Today, we live as the embodiment of the significant events that created our recollections.

Read, recollect and relive the joy, the excitement, the wonder of those unique moments in your history that made the who of you.

Is It a Memory or a Recollection?

Some folks use the words "memory" and "recollection" as interchangeable expressions of recall. To me, that's like saying red-orange is close enough to red to be used for red. That assertion bends my mind, as does using the word memory for recollection.

In my mind, a memory is a snapshot of a past event. The picture shows a one-dimensional view of a precious day-gone-by. It shows, for instance, an old-fashioned pump in the farmyard, and one remembers drinking from the dipper that hung on the pump. The memory evokes a smile and maybe a "Do you guys remember our trip to the farm?" A memory is the "make nice" piece of our mind.

A recollection, to my mind, is the story of an influential or monumental event that we share because recollections are significant. You can feel how it impacted your life when the event happened and as you retell it as a story with your family and friends. Consider, for instance, how the snapshot of the pump in the yard differs from the full recollection of that episode.

As you recollect that drink, you also recall your thirst and how you got that drink. You feel the hard metal pump handle in your hand and the resistance as you pull the handle up and push it down. You feel your impatience as you continue to pump and nothing is happening. You listen intently for the sound of water rising in the pipe. You push a little harder, a little faster as you hear the water rising. You continue to pump. Finally, the water pulses from the gaping pump mouth into the bucket below. You continue to pump to purge the water left standing in the pipe and reach for the big, blue-and-white speckled, long-handled enameled dipper. You give the pump handle one more hefty downward push. The water flows, and you slide the dipper into the stream. You anticipate the cool taste of the fresh, cold water stored hundreds of feet down in the earth. You stop pumping and savor the freshness, the coldness in your throat. You drink long and deeply and sigh an "Ah," as you wipe a couple of drops from your lips with the back of your hand. Satisfied, you hang the dipper back on the makeshift hook on the pump. You turn and leave.

When you leave, you walk away with a memory of the day you pumped a drink of fresh, cool water for yourself.

Life on the Mountain Trail

Toward the fog she pointed her
Nikon. Intrigued by the fading view,

she pressed the shutter button,
hopeful her lens had captured on film

what she saw in the silence. She heard the
shutter close its mind on the scene. Later a

metaphor for life lay in the developing tray,
the mystery coming into focus, cell by silver cell.

Emerging images drew her eye into the frame.
Today, visible in the foreground puddle, the rain

droplets on the wood railing coax the viewer to
follow the mountain pathway. Hints of tomorrow

lay as beckoning shadows in the mist. Still, the
riddle of the foggy impressions ahead promises

to reveal itself   if the hiker follows   the niggling
lure of discovery   with just   one more   damp step.

Racing Down Deadman's Hill

We fearless sled riders never called it Deadman's Hill, but after one afternoon of crazy sledding on that hill, I thought it easily could become that name.

For most of the winter, six or eight of us grade schoolers, between the ages of eight and 12, would drag our Flexible Flyer sleds down 11-Mile Road, past my Grandmother Kent's house, to Putnam's Hill. The basic group of sled riders—Ricky, Billy, Allen, Clifford and me—met at the bottom of my grandmother's hill. Other riders came and went, depending on the weather. From Grandma Kent's house, we talked little and hurried along toward the hill, about a half mile away.

We stepped on the flattened, rusted wire fence, bumping our sleds over behind us, and marched a few yards to the top of the hill. This hill had a long, wide slope toward Grand River, the main highway between Detroit and Lansing. Big, tall trees dotted the landscape on either side of the slope.

One winter, our ordinary playfulness changed from individual head-to-head races and competitive downhill heats to something more sinister. Sometimes we were too inventive for our own good. Maybe it had something to do with our getting older, but not wiser. This became one of those times.

Generally, we made great sport of starting with two or three racers (depending upon the number of participants we had) at the top of the hill. We raucously launched the race with a loud, "GO!" The racers, hands on sleds, ran along side of their Flyers and flopped aboard when they felt ready. Racers took turns standing watch at the bottom of the hill to determine the winner of the heat. We competed in a spirit of friendship, not rules. Sure, we had our squabbles, but we wanted to race our sleds, so we quickly settled that nonsense. The speed was exhilarating, excitement ran high.

We stayed on the hill until the sun dropped behind the trees and sent long shadows over our raceway. The length of the shadows was the signal that our moms would be expecting us home for supper. very soon.

Over our hours of daily racing, the hill gained an icy sheen, and the races grew faster. The speed was exhilarating; excitement ran high.

Nevertheless, Ricky, the daredevil in our group (there always is one), wanted to do more. He thought it would be fun to make a line of sleds and weave among the tall, dark trees that had witnessed our many races.

Sounded like a good idea at the time.

I was the lead sled in the first downhill run. I hooked my black-booted toes into the steering loop of the sled behind me. Each sled rider did the same, until all sleds—six of us—were connected. Then we pushed off.

Together, we sort of paddled our way down the hill to gain some momentum. Within seconds, our line of sleds was weaving downhill among the sturdy trees, through fresh, soft, white snow, which kept our early trips under control. As the lead sled, I kept the line of travel fairly straight through the trees the first time through. I was not a fan of crack-the-whip games.

We laughed and shouted with the speed, the wind, and the excitement of racing among the towering trees. When we slowed to a stop at the bottom of the hill, the motorists on Grand River, who had watched our trip downhill as they waited at the traffic light, honked and waved out rolled-down windows. We waved back and turned to trudge up the hill for another run.

After the second run, I dropped back to the last-sled position. Something had been bothering me about this game since the first run, and I wanted a fresh perspective. (No one would have suspected me of being a mother hen, but I was.) As we zoomed down the hill on the third run, I realized that we were playing a really deadly version of crack-the-whip: Six loaded sleds whipping around the trees, gaining speed, young riders engaged in careless fun was a scary possibility.

Weaving around the huge trees at an ever-increasing speed was treacherous folly. The last two or three sled riders were in danger. If the leader of the pack became too daring, or riders weren't paying attention, the end of the whip could slam into a tree and the rider be seriously hurt. Or worse.

I was the eldest of the lot, which isn't saying much. I was 12 years old, a responsible 12-year-old. My Grandmother, whom I always stopped to see on my way to the hill, reminded me that when I was the eldest of the bunch, I needed to pay attention to the little ones in the group. Be sure they were up to what we older ones planned to do. "Little ones are not fast thinkers. You need to think for them." She told me. "Yes, Gramma," She knew I would.

After the second run, those little ones in our group were top on my mind. "Hey, guys. What do you say we run two whips? One on this side of the hill and another over there, on the other side of our raceway. That way nobody will be standing around, waiting for a turn."

Clifford, one of the younger boys, said, "Yeah! Let's do that!" Later, he said, quietly, that the last time we went down in the long line, it really scared him.

"Me, too." I thought. Man, I truly didn't want an accident to turn our winter playground into Deadman's Hill. If any of us had gotten hurt, even a little bit, the adults would never let us come back. Then what would we do?

All names have been changed to protect the unsuspecting, in case they have not yet gone on to greener pastures.

Learning at the Seat of Contempt

Friends invited our family to a snazzy company-sponsored retreat in the country one summer. The place had pleasant cabins tucked among acres of trees that surrounded a very big lake. The dad in other family worked as an executive in a major business-machine corporation that rewarded its executives with vacation time at "The Farm." The company allowed executives to invite friends to the facility.

I never thought of our families—the Sinclairs and the Snows—as being friends. I was in the same grade as their daughter, Donna, and our moms volunteered in the community and belonged to a couple of the same social groups. But my dad was a factory worker, not a neat-and-tidy executive like Mr. Sinclair. When my dad came home, his clothes were dirty and, often, his hands were cut up and ugly from a miscue at the lathe he used to trim the pieces of metal that he shaped. Once in a while, the adults in several local families, including mine, would get together to play pinochle, but that was pretty much it.

Basically, the only thing the families had in common was us kids—three girls, three boys collectively.

The deal for this vacation was that my family would stay in a cabin separate from theirs, but we would share potluck evening meals on their screened porch.

This story is important to me because the event changed the lives in my household. For sure, that week drastically changed the behaviors of my two brothers and me. We were transformed from constant adversaries who squabbled about anything and over anything into decent siblings. Compared to the cruel children we spent that week with, my brothers and I would qualify as angels.

We arrived at The Farm on Sunday evening, which was spent exploring our cabin and its surroundings. Then, while the adults talked, we girls investigated the possibilities for the next day. For openers, we made plans to go rowing in the morning. Our rowing exceeded the morning, however. Donna, Christy, and I spent hours rowing and hiking around this enormous, interesting lake. We talked and talked and laughed and kept rowing and hiking. I had no idea what the boys were doing. Didn't much care, either.

The impetus for our post-vacation transformation began to take shape during the times our families were together. As a rule, my brothers and I argued and fussed and fumed and drove our parents to distractions, as adults are given to saying. As combative as we were at home, nothing we had done even came close to the shock of the family time experience with the Sinclairs. Their family was the epitome of "all is not as it seems."

Mr. and Mrs. Sinclair were both super involved in their Baptist church. The rules of their church were very important to them. "Upstanding members" of the church was how they were talked about in the community. As a 12-year-old kid, I thought their church participation was more of a mystery. For instance, although I never saw evidence of this myself, but their "love of the drink" was well known throughout the community. I also thought they were just kind of stuffy, maybe even uppity to tell the truth.

The church stuff never spilled over into my relationship with the girls. Donna and I played jacks in the winter and roller skated around and around the school during the spring. Their younger girl, Christy, was a friend, too. We never did anything special, but, from time to time, we had fun together. The boy, Ricky, was much younger and a real pain, a smart mouth who had to be in the middle of everything, even if the conversation or event had nothing to do with him. And, like my brothers, Ricky could do no wrong.

Anyway, we all gathered at the Sinclair's cabin for

our casual potluck supper Sunday on the screened porch. Nothing fancy. Hamburgers, hot dogs, potato salad, chips. All the important stuff. Then it started.

"Ricky, bring the napkins from the kitchen." Mrs. S. said. No "please" attached. Ricky was maybe nine years old.

Ricky: "You do it. I'm hungry, and I'm not your slave.

What's wrong with this picture? Ricky's being disrespectful to his mother and Mr. S. isn't correcting him? Mrs. S. went for the napkins.

Mr. S.: "Christy, would you get the ketchup? Your mother forgot it." Huh? It doesn't matter who forgot the ketchup, but Mr. S. had to lay blame on Mrs. S. Furthermore, he was not about to get the ketchup himself. He was too cool to move.

"How can anyone be so stupid?" Christy said, as she walked away. "She should get it. She forgot it."

Why did Mrs. S. put up with comments like those? And how does any kid get away with speaking about a parent that way.

What is this? Beat up on Mrs. S. night? Not to put too fine a point on this, but the kids were rude and obnoxious to their mother throughout the rest of the meal. Besides that, Mr. S. did nothing in defense of his wife or to curtail his children's rudeness. My brothers and I sat dumbfounded. Man, if any of the three of us had ever spoken to our mom like that, Dad would have taken the offending child outside for a good "talking to."

We looked to our parents for direction. What we got was the stern "keep your mouth shut" look.

I would like to say that this experience in abusive behavior was a one-off, but it sure as the dickens was not. The Snow family shared two more joint meals with the Sinclairs. Each was prickly with disrespect from the children and disinterest from Mr. S. It was like he couldn't be bothered with anyone or anything, unless it pertained to him. Somehow, our potlucks ended, and we Snows ate on our own screened porch. We ate quietly. None of us said a word about anything we had seen and heard on the other porch. Those evenings had been way too unbelievable to think about, much less speak about out loud, in real words.

The result of our experience was this: My brothers and I might occasionally get snarky in a touchy moment, but the week with the Sinclairs was so stunning in its offensiveness that our being nice to one another became routine, and the responding "please" and "thank you" were nearly overdone.

To this day, more than 60 years later, the words and the pictures of the exchanges between those children and their mother are just as vivid and as disgusting as in the days I lived through them. Just as clear and reprehensible, too, is the image of Mr. S., sitting so prim and proper, smug and aloof as his bratty, spoiled children disrespected his wife of many years.

The girls and I continued to get along in school. We weren't quite so chummy as we used to be, but we did get along. Moreover, I surely didn't think so much of Mr. S. He was an adult not to be trusted. Even if he was a big deal in his church.

Humility and Pride

We were smack in the middle of basketball season, and our girls' team was playing our school's biggest rival. The scoring was fairly one sided. Our team was ahead by 16 points; the number of points I had scored in the first half.

As we rested at the half, I made what I thought was a simple observation about the score to my best friend, Nancy.

"If I weren't playing, the score would be tied." My comment was intended as nothing more than noticing the mathematical fact. Nancy took the statement as something much different, however.

"Well! I guess you think you're so damn good, you don't need the rest of the team." She was intense and loud.

I was gobsmacked.

First of all, Nancy rarely spoke so pointedly. She didn't raise her voice, much less cuss. Second, she was quite right in her criticism. Although I had not intended my comment as such, she perceived it as pure hubris. I understood and was sorely embarrassed.

I did not consider myself to be any special kind of athlete. Yes, I practiced hard and took some satisfaction in my growth in skills and accomplishments. I knew, for instance, when an opposing player was going to pass the ball and to whom. I watched eyes and body language. I anticipated the moment to break for the target, steal the ball, and dribble in for a successful layup. That was an innate gift that no amount of practice can produce.

The gift of that innate skill belonged to God. He had gifted me with intuition, high reaction time, and the love of the contest, always. I took no credit ever for His gifts. But I reveled in how good it felt when those skills came together.

That day on the basketball court taught me a critical life-long lesson: Think before you speak, and when you speak, credit others first and foremost. Thank them for their hard work and dedication to the health and success of the team, whatever kind of team claims you and your spirit.

The Stain of Impulse

It has been a harrowing week in the homestead. My husband is traveling in Iowa, gone the whole week. Gratefully, my girls, Laurie and Sharon, are in school. Tim, my precocious three-year-old, still tests me throughout the day. Thank the Lord for naptime.

One more night alone at dinnertime with the kids, however.

I have finally finished painting the kitchen/dining area, and I am a pooped painter. The west-facing room had been a warm peach color, which added to the heat of meal preparation. I opted for a cool blue, which I applied whenever the kids were otherwise occupied. It was tough keeping the tools of the project at the ready. However, I had the will and the way to make it happen. Windows on two sides of the room let in loads of light. Over at least a week or so, I cleaned and painted the half shutters and hung fresh white valances, with satin-stitched eyelets.

The greatest challenge of this project was the ceiling. In the 50s, when our house was built, the bumpy popcorn ceilings were the "in" thing. A ceiling with white chicken pox, as it were. It looked okay, but it has been a bear to paint. No matter how fluffy the paint roller, the rough surface required critical diligence to be sure the surface was fully covered. I am not good with tedious tasks, and this task is tediousness, with a capital T. This infernal ceiling has made me reconsider all future painting projects on my list.

As with most Mom projects, my painting has been confined to the hours when Tim was in his playpen or napping and, then, as soon as I settled the kids at night. My tools were ready to roll when I could. My painting ended yesterday.

As I shaped the burgers and spilled t frozen French fries onto a cookie sheet, ready for the oven, I asked Laurie to set the table and Sharon to get the condiments and cheese from the fridge. Tim is running back and forth, getting in their way. Basically, he is tormenting Sharon as she tries to do as I asked. She can get only one thing from the fridge at a time because she is a little five-year-old and her big horn-rimmed glasses keep sliding down on her nose and distracting her. The tormenting and squabbling continued as I finished the burgers and spread ketchup on Tim's burger. Despite my requests for them to cease and desist, they persisted with their nonsense.

Finally, my last Mom nerve snapped.

I slammed the ketchup bottle in my hand down hard on the table. "Confound it!" I shouted, as I did so. Before you say, "Oh, no! Don't tell me . . .," just pretend that I am not telling you this. Yes, a big glob of ketchup was air-locked in the tall neck of the bottle. And, yes, when I smacked that bottle on the table, the force launched a thick, gooey glob straight up and onto my freshly painted *white* popcorn ceiling. What started as a one-inch glob splattered generously over those popcorn bumps.

I stood there, staring at the drooping goop, waiting for it to fall onto the table. But, no, the Heinz® slow, oozing thickness just hung there, defying gravity. Waggling an imaginary red finger at me for my vigorous impulsiveness.

Then, I looked at the kids, who were wide-eyed and petrified. What was momma going to do? Would she holler at them? They looked terrified.

I threw my hands up, then smacked my thighs with them, and said, as I turned my attention from the goop on the ceiling to the kids, "Well, what do you think of that? Pretty dumb, huh?" The kids broke into the raucous laughter of relief. I laughed, too. What else does one do in such a situation?

The ketchup clean-up would have to wait until the next day. Or maybe the one after that. I was too tired to do more than tidy the dinner debris and put the kids to bed. The thought of hauling the ladder from the shed to the kitchen was too much.

Tediousness struck again. Cleaning the splat of thick ketchup from the chicken pox took nearly as long as it did to paint the entire ceiling. And because the new paint had not cured, the goo left a faint hint of pink among the bumps, no matter how diligently I scrubbed. I decided not to paint over the pink. The stain served as a reminder that a moment of thought before engaging in impulsive behavior is the wiser decision.

The Case of the Talking Nose

"Don't cry because it's over, smile because it happened." Dr. Seuss offered his readers dozens upon dozens of lessons in his wonderful stories. The quote above, which I entered into the conversation with my friends, is my favorite. Somehow, the simplicity of this thought always makes any sad situation better. We had been sharing a moment of sadness of loss.

As we women talked, pictures of a favorite story time came to mind. (I am not given to lingering on sad times.) My children loved Dr. Seuss books at bedtime, especially *Fox in Sox*, which I read often because we all loved his fun, musical language. So, as was our custom after bath time, we—Sharon, six, Tim, four, and Dan three— cuddled close on the couch in our family room for my very dramatic reading of *Fox in Sox*. Laurie, 11, decided that she was too old for story hour, but I knew she was listening on the sofa in the living room. She loved stories.

•. •. •. •. •.

So, let's join Mr. Fox as he tells Mr. Knox this tongue twister of a story.

> *"Clocks on fox tick.*
> *Clocks on Knox tock.*
> *Six sick bricks tick.*
> *Six sick chicks tock.*

> *"Please, sir. I don't like this trick, sir.*
> *"My tongue isn't quick or slick, sir."*

The children and I were rocking right along in Dr. Seuss's clever rhymes. The children listened intently.

> *"New socks. Two socks. Whose socks? Sue's socks.*
> *Who sews Sue's socks? Sue sews Sue's socks."*

I was on a roll with the rhymes until I got to this . . .

> *"Through three cheese trees three free fleas flew . . ."*

From the corner of my eye I could see Tim staring at me intensely. He suddenly burst out with one of those front-of-the-mouth sounds, the one that sounds like a stifled laugh, and he bent over his outstretched legs. Then he giggled a bit.

"Tim, honey, sit up so we can finish the story," I said, as I slipped my hand around his shoulder and helped him sit up. He turned and looked at me and did another front-of-the-mouth burst. But he settled. I patted his leg, as mothers are wont to do, to thank him. I began again, using my best voice and reading style.

> " . . . *Through three cheese trees three free fleas flew.*
> *While these fleas flew, freezy breeze blew . . .*"

I could see that Tim still was watching me. He strained to be quiet and attentive until I got to the next tongue-twister section, one of the best in the book, from my perspective.

> "*Let's have a little talk about tweetle beetles.*
> *What do you know about tweetle beetles?*
> *Well, when tweetle beetles fight,*
> *it's called a tweetle beetle battle.*
> *And when they battle in a puddle,*
> *it's called a tweetle beetle puddle battle.*
> *AND when tweetle beetles . . .*"

Tim erupted into total laughter, bending in half and laying his head on his brown-and-white-plaid pajama-covered knees. ("Dang! I wish I could do that," I thought.) Now, I know I am no beauty queen, but I also think my face is not a laughing matter.

"Tim David! What in the world is so funny? Sit up here and tell me." I was right on the high side of grumpy at this point. I took hold of his shoulders and sat him upright. The other two children were sitting there, puzzled by Tim's behavior and getting a bit fidgety with these delays.

He looked up at me, stifled another laugh, and said, "Your nose talks!" Again, he fell into a gale of laughter and buried his face into his outstretched legs.

"What?"

He raised up a bit and turned toward me. "Your nose talks when you read." More laughter.

I had no idea what he was telling me. "Okay. Okay," I said, as I gave him a quick hug. "Let's just finish the book. Sharon and Dan are getting tired, and it's time for all of you to be in bed. Just look at the pictures in the book, not at me, until we are done. Deal?" Fortunately, the tweetle beetles were near the end of the story, and I was able to finish quickly.

After I got them tucked into bed, I stopped in the bathroom. My nose talks? I looked into the mirror and recited some lines from the story.

"By George, the boy is right. The end of my nose bobs when I talk." That is a story-ending revelation.

Beauregard the Beagle Hound

A few years back, I visited family friends on Daniel Island, SC. As the host served morning tea, he told me that our tea was from this one-of-a-kind tea plantation on Wadmalaw Island, southwest of Charleston. I visited the plantation on my way back to Florida. All of the pieces in here were part of my visit. I rearranged them and wrote this story for Caleb, their very brainy seven-year-old boy.

This is the story of Beauregard, a tri-colored beagle hound, who lives on a farm. Not just any farm, however. He lives on the Charleston Tea Plantation, the only tea farm in America. Beauregard's master grows hundreds and hundreds and hundreds of tea bushes on Wadmalaw Island in South Carolina. These bushes grow very special, small, light-green leaves on their tops. After the leaves are picked, they go into the tea factory where they are dried and made even more special. They become so special, in fact, that when someone pours boiling-hot water over these leaves in a cup or in a teapot, they make a brownish-yellow drink called "tea."

Anyway, young Beauregard is a frisky hound who is not interested in drinking tea. However, he does love to run and sniff along the ground, because that's what a hound dog does. He runs and sniffs and hunts with his sensitive dog nose.

Each morning, Beauregard impatiently pushes his nose against the wooden front gate until his master lifts the latch and swings the gate open. Beauregard shoves hard through the first crack and makes the gate swing wide. He races to the tea fields as fast as his short legs can go. His long, floppy ears flap up and down as he bounds through the weedy field toward the long hedgerows of tea bushes.

When Beauregard reaches the tea bushes, he begins to sniff the ground. He runs here and there. He runs there, and he runs here. He sniffs, his nose close to the ground, while he scampers.

Sniff.

Sniff, sniff.

Sniff, sniff, sniff.

From one row to another.

Beauregard stops, raises a white paw, and pauses.

"Beauregard! Come!" His master's sharp commands blow on the wind from the farmhouse to the tea bushes.

"Thweeeeet! Thweeeeet!" Beauregard knows that sound. That's the master's sharp whistle, and when the master whistles, Beauregard should run back to the farmhouse. But he so loves to run among the tea bushes. His master's shrill whistle is soon followed by another shouted command. "Beauregard! Get back here!" His master sounds really unhappy.

Beauregard stands very still and raises his yellowish-brown head. His body quivers a moment in response to his master's firm demand. He hears his master, but he is not ready to return home.

His nose twitches as he sniffs the morning air. He does not see what he wants, and he does not yet smell it. He puts paw and nose to the ground again and runs off. He runs farther along and into the hedgerows of tea bushes, and he sniffs and sniffs.

Suddenly, Beauregard snorts and sneezes and shakes his head. His tawny ears flip and flap. He sneezes and sneezes. Something Beauregard sniffed did not please, and he starts to sneeze. He rubs a paw across his nose and returns to his sniffing puzzle.

Beauregard disappears among the low branches, where he sniffs and sniffs. He is still sniffing when he pops out of the rows and searches with his eyes, not his nose. His master is closer now.

"Beauregard! Come here!" His master claps his hands twice, sharply, and Beauregard knows his nose must follow his ears to keep his master happy.

Beauregard hunts for something that his keen eyes never spy. Alas, Beauregard the beagle hound never found what he sought on the ground around the tea bushes. The hound never found a Tea-Bone on the tea-bushes ground.

Our Adventure in the Circle of Life

My family and I had moved to a small farming community in Orion, IL, in the late 60s. The move was quite a change. We had lived in an orderly residential area in Michigan for 10 years or so. You know, one of those places with neat brick homes, sidewalks, a school nearby, and our mail was tucked into the mailbox on the house six days a week.

The town of Orion, however, sits on a hill in the middle of its 1,800 residents (1,806 some 40 years later, the research shows), hog farms, and cornfields. No matter from which direction one approaches the town, every roadway descends into the valley that embraces the town. All of the commerce exists on that hill or leading to its crest. I mention this because I want you to know that Orion really was a funky, nice place before the corn field takes over the story.

We had moved to this predominately Swedish community because my husband was starting a job as a salesman for a major machine manufacturing company. He would be selling these machines in Illinois and across the Rock River into Iowa. This was an exciting opportunity for him because the machine he was selling was an early version of computer-controlled machinery. His market was farm-equipment manufacturers.

That we had moved to a friendly community was important to me. For the first time in my life, I would be hundreds of miles from my family. Family had always been close. Growing up, I had often stayed overnight with my cousins. And I had spent weeks at a time on my grandparents' farm in central Michigan in the summer. Regular family gatherings, with 15 or 20 grandparents, aunts, uncles, cousins present, sometimes more, were common. Regular family time of some kind was routine.

Now, my four young, small children and I had to establish new relationships with the community and its people. No neat sidewalks. And the mail was in the post office in Orion, on the hill a mile and a half from the house. I sometimes skipped the trip to the post office in the winter. Until the salt was spread, the icy hill could be tricky.

We had bought a beautiful brick home in a clean, well-kept neighborhood on the corner of 12th Avenue and 13th Street. The entire block behind the houses was a huge open area. No fences spoiled the landscape. All of the blocks were this way.

On the corner across the street from us lay one of those ubiquitous seed-corn fields that were snugged up against nearly every fence line along U.S.150, from the Orion to Peoria. The cornfield kitty corner from the house stretched way off into the distance. I had grown up on a small farm, so farmland was a welcome touchstone in the newness.

We had moved into our home at the beginning of summer when the corn was green and tall. Now, the corn stalks were turning brown and drying out. Just before Halloween, the farmer roared into the field to harvest the seed corn. He drove the biggest John Deere tractor I had ever seen. It stood taller than our house and was nearly as big.

This monster John Deere entering the field also had a device on the front, a corn harvester, that cut the dried stalks a foot from the ground and separated the cobs from the stalks. The harvester spit the cobs into the bed of a truck that followed alongside of the harvester. The stalks were spewed onto the field.

As the farmer cleared the field over the next day or two, I began to notice the occasional mouse scurrying across the kitchen counter. Not good. Time to get some mouse traps.

I went up to the hardware in the town square on the hill and asked Rodney, the owner/manager of the business for a couple of mouse traps. Actually, I bought a half dozen traps. Just to be sure.

"Are you sure that's enough?" He asked. A sly smile teased the corners of his mouth, as he questioned me. A twinkle of mischief shone in his smiling eyes.

"I think so. I haven't seen many mice." I replied. Rodney smiled, again.

Rodney clearly knew that I was a greenhorn, pretty inexperienced in the trials of living in big-time farm country. Nevertheless, I should have remembered my days in the hayfield at harvest time on Grandpa Snow's farm. We children would run along the rows of freshly harvested hay and hoot with joy when we turned over nest after nest of tiny, hairless mice under those hay rows.

Anyway, I set four traps that afternoon.

I had barely stepped away, when I heard the traps snap. Of course, I disposed of the critters and reset the traps. Before bedtime, I heard "Snap!   Snap! Snap! Snap!" I added the two other traps.

Soon, I began to see more and more mice in the kitchen and laundry room. And then in the book-lined den. Any place where it was warm and had food or nesting materials. Mice loved paper for their nests.

As I read to the children before bed, I could hear mice scurrying. They love to play at night. One time, when I was standing quietly in the kitchen, I saw little mouse ears poking up around the burners in my gas-powered range. And other mice boldly scooted across the countertop. It was getting a little unnerving, this invasion of rodents.

One morning, my older daughter, Laurie, went to the kitchen for a glass of milk.

Suddenly, she screamed and ran to her bedroom.

I hurried to the kitchen and then to her bedroom to see what the commotion was all about. Well, a mouse had run across her toes, as she was pouring her milk. Clearly, I had to take far better defensive actions to get rid of those rodents before they overtook the house, and we had more than spilled milk.

The next day, I returned to the hardware store for more mouse traps. It appeared that the mice had begun a takeover.

I was quite familiar with the bother of mice in the house. I had lived in the country all my life, and mice are just part of God's circle of life in the country. Just not in my house and most certainly not to this extent.

This onslaught was akin to some slick sales mouse organizing a block-grant family relocation event in the field on the corner. "Tired of living the uncertain Country Field Mouse life? Move on up. Cross over the road to a better way of living. City House Mouse warmth is there for the taking. Some hazards and cautions may apply."

I returned to the hardware three times over the next couple of weeks, picking up two or three more traps each time, and, each time, just as hopeful that I had purchased enough. Alas, the collection numbered 18 traps when I ran out of room to set them. I strung them out in suspected travel areas through the kitchen, laundry room, and the den full of books. Away from little fingers and hands, of course.

During the first week of trapping, I loaded the six traps with cheese and baloney (mice seemed to love the greasy luncheon meat). I cleared the trap line a couple of times a day. The scurrying still bugged me, though. Hence, the additional traps.

As I read to the children each night, I kept hearing the Snap! Snap, snap, snap! Snap!

Then, after I tucked the kids into bed, I checked the traps. Well, to make a long story a whole lot shorter, I trapped 34 mice during the first week, 30 the next week, and fewer each week. No trap went untouched by an inquisitive mouse. I was an equal opportunity trapper.

By the time that winter was over, I finally had a mouse-free house. We had trapped way more than 100 mice over that fall and winter. I had grown weary of and disgusted by the routine of emptying the traps and stopped counting the trophies.

My children had joined into the game of "trap the mouses," too. When they heard the traps "snap," one of them would holler "mouse" and run to get the rubber gloves I used, taking care to handle them by the cuffs. It was not the best of games, but it was better than making mouse trapping an ugly experience. As I said, mice are just a part of living in farm country. Gratefully, we were so diligent the mice never had the chance to reproduce. Or if they did, the evidence was missing.

The good news here is this: The school district had bought that corn field for a high school. By the next fall, the new school was under construction, and I did not have to play the great mouse hunter again. I do think, however, that the younger children missed their "trap the mouses" adventure.

A Spider Broke My Heart

One night she was there, the next morning she was gone. And so was her web. Only three radial strands remained. I was stunned. I had inspected her intricate web nearly every day for a week or so, and suddenly she was gone.

I know that Spiny (I named her because she had become a friend) was a "she" because the spider-wise guys write that the male spine-backed orb-web weaver like Spiny does not weave webs. He only hunts for mates. Nothing new there.

Anyway, this spider wove a web that was as lacy as the spider was sort of clunky-looking. Her body was slightly larger than a fat M&M. What I see is her abdomen, not her back, which looks like a Halloween cookie: white with black dots arranged to look like a face—small dots at the upper edge resemble a hair line, two larger dots for eye, two smaller dots for nostrils, and several small dots for a broad smile. Six red, cone-shaped spines, arranged equidistant from one corner of the smile to the other, protrude from the side of her abdomen.

Spiny and her web had hung around my porch for several weeks, and I was accustomed to and enjoyed seeing her when I walked to my car.

As I left for my shift at Tidewell Hospice House one morning, I had seen a spider beginning to weave its web. It had spun three radial strands from the roof overhang to a plastic garbage can that I used for clippings and weeds, just outside of my screened porch. While I was gone, the spider added other radials, like spokes in a wheel. Now, as I watched, it began to add the concentric circles that characterize the spiny-orb web. This is when I checked with the spider-wise guys online, and when I learned that Spiny was female.

Once her work was done, Spiny positioned herself in the center of her orb, which was somewhat larger than a dinner plate. Her Halloween decorated tummy showed prominently. On her web, a white substance appeared on the radial strands in an equidistant manner, like the lane markings on a roadway. The spider-wise guys believe that these white dashes catch the light and call attention to the web.

Over the course of her stay, the web would sometimes have wide bare spots. The bare spots puzzled me, but she always filled them within a short time. The pattern remained concentric circles, but neat variations had been added. The variations were, I learned, the product of necessity. Overall, the measurements remained consistent between the parallel lines. This puzzled me, too.

Well, the spider-wise guys say that the weaver's design is directly proportional to the distance from the tip of her back legs to her spinneret, which is at the center of her hind body.

The voids appeared in the web because the spiny orb eats portions of its web every day. To conserve energy, it recycles the protein in the silk. With each recycling, the web design varied. The modifications always were dainty—lace-doily like.

Nearly every day, I had stopped and looked, amazed by what this creature could do and had done every day.

I guess this was the rub for Spiny. I had invaded her comfort zone and peered at her workmanship too often.

One morning, as I left the porch, the absence of ever-present web, sparkling in the morning sunlight, startled me. Only three radial strands remained. She had eaten her web and left.

I was stunned again. It was kind of like my best friend had died unexpectedly. I sucked in a gulp of air, checked the scene carefully. Don't you know, I nearly cried. The unkindest cut of all came the next morning. The three radial strands were gone, too. Not pulled or broken and left blowing in the wind. Just gone.

It was like Spiny had pitched a fit, left home, and returned in the dark of night for the rest of her things. My friend had walked out on me and slammed the door in my mind. Harsh.

The Power of Odd

The odd number three,
the lonely one
and pent up five

    add odd interest
    to any gathering
    of elements

    be they words,
    birds or vases
    or maybe cases

        of exquisite wine.
        Artists pursue
        odd numbers to give

        their works motion
        and interest that fails
        with numbers like

two or four or
evens more. They bore.
Odd motivates imagination.

The Pots and the Kettle

A friend and I were shopping at the local mall. Shopping is not a favorite pastime for me, but I did enjoy time with my friend, so I accompanied her to the mall. She wanted to shop in the Hallmark store; I declined to join her. The card store had way too much visual input in a confined space for me. Instead, I sat on one of the benches on the pedestrian mall.

To my right was the kiosk full of the newest craze—mobile phones. A young man, maybe in his twenties, was inspecting phone after phone, looking for just the right one. Small, free-standing cell phones had just become the invention novelty of the week, and this booth had a resplendent assortment of designs and colors.

I had noticed this fellow because he had turned his blond hair into a neon-green cactus look. Green spikes all over his head above the blond fringe. The boldness of color mesmerized me. He and the blaze of small phones seemed well suited to each other.

Our neon-cactus fellow also had caught the attention of a couple of vintage biker dudes walking through the mall.

One of the men, a trim looking fellow of about 55, wore a T-shirt and shorts. His shirt had been modified by ripping off the sleeves and leaving ragged arm holes. The frayed shorts were cut offs, from which very hairy legs disappeared into black Harley socks and boots. I know that they were Harley products because the logo appeared on both. He wore wire-rimmed glasses, had an unkempt mustache, and a faux American flag do rag on his balding head.

The other guy was about the same age and sported the obligatory ponytail and heavy chain that drooped from a belt loop to secure his billfold in his hip pocket. His chest hair curled over the neck of his sleeveless undershirt. The hair on his shoulders and the back of his neck also curled around his garment. A belt of bare belly peeked out between his well-stretched undershirt and well-worn jeans.

Tough-guy tattoos adorned most of the open areas on arms and legs on both men.

The two were doing their best biker-dude power strut down the mall. Slow, with purpose and just the right amount of swagger. As they approached the kiosk and the young neon-cactus man, they just stared as they passed, giving him long, disapproving looks as they sashayed by. They practically walked backward in their effort to take a good look and deliver their disparaging message. However, the neon cactus did not notice, or maybe he ignored, their disapproval.

Their curiosity sated, the do-rag dude smacks the ponytail in the chest with the back of his hand and said in total disbelief, "Can you imagine doing anything like that to yourself?"

"Nah," the ponytail replies. "My old lady would kill me if I did anything so stupid."

Drum roll and cymbal crash—the pots exit stage left, leaving the kettle on stage, holding his psychedelic green-and-pink phone.

You Must Leave Now!

The ski lift intrigued me. Idly, I probed my chicken salad with my fork. Chair after empty chair slowly rises above the tree-filled, rock-dotted, grassy terrain toward the ski lodge on Sandia Peak, a tiny dot at the top of the mountain.

Young people carrying mountain bikes step onto the painted footprints and wait for a chair to slide under them. In constant motion upward, they and their bikes head toward their thrill ride downhill. If I were a young person living here, I probably would be doing as they, riding upward, watching the terrain, and plotting my downhill ride. What a great day for such an adventure

It is July in New Mexico, and the ski lift makes possible an adventurous summer for daring bicycle riders and people who just want to explore. For the fee of $10 per rider, the bikers ride chairs up the 31km (a little more than 19 miles) to the ski lodge. The lodge is not their destination, however; it is merely a stop-over. Once they set their bikes on the ground, they will launch themselves onto the 19-mile downhill obstacle course to test their reflexes and their courage, racing around rocks, leaping over low-lying logs and avoiding other obstacles, as other chairs glide by overhead.

I continued to be distracted. My thoughts lingered on the rhythmic swing of the chairs. A sound in the small restaurant broke my concentration, and I blurted, "How do you feel about taking a ride up the mountain to the ski lodge?" I surprised myself with the question. I nodded toward the window. It was a glorious, clear day, and we were enjoying free time scheduled into our conference itinerary.

She turned her attention toward the ski lift. "I don't know. It looks pretty far away."

"You aren't going to walk to the top," I answered impatiently. "You are riding. What difference does the distance make?"

"Well, maybe it would be an interesting change." She answered. Her voice lacked enthusiasm.

"Sounds like a 'no' to me, girl. Let's go back to Albuquerque and walk around. I'm good with that." I took a long drink of my iced tea.

"No, let's do it! It's good to break out of our ruts." Now, she sounded almost enthusiastic.

We finished our lunch and went to the ski-lift admission hut. We paid our $10 fee per person and, as directed, stood on the yellow footprints painted onto the concrete platform. A wooden chair bumped the backs of our thighs, and we plopped down onto it.

We began our herky-jerky trip toward the peak (herky-jerky because the riders were few and far between)—and our surprise adventure.

"Wait!" My friend cried out in distress after she fastened the thin black lap restraint. "I am claustrophobic! I am trapped! Sing to me." She implored. "Sing something."

Sing? Her strange demand startled me.

"Distract me, please. I'm afraid." She urged.

A hymn popped into my mind, and I began, "I come to the garden alone, while the dew is still on the roses, and the voice I hear falling on my ear . . ." This definitely was not the time for "The hills are alive with the sound of music," which I would have preferred to sing. So I sang hymns from my childhood. She didn't comment on my singing. That was okay with me. So long as she stopped being frantic, I would sing.

•. •. •. •. •.

We bumped along unevenly, and the lodge became more visible. Suddenly, a cool wind blew across our fretful ride. Its intensity grew and drops of rain intruded. The rain surged and grew into dime-size hail. The pounding hail surprised us. The hail increased in intensity, but not in size, gratefully.

We hunched and raised our arms to protect our heads. We were exposed, totally vulnerable, hanging out in space. The pounding of the hail was more irritating than hurtful, although a few icy pellets stung my back and shoulders. My friend's fear and my singing were replaced by apprehension and agitation. The elements persisted. The ski lodge still lay several minutes away.

Finally, our chair cleared the platform at the ski lodge. Soaked through our clothes, we lunged from our seats and raced toward the lodge and piles of paper towels. The predictable blow dryers were useless, but we found a stack of paper towels and blotted the worst of the wetness from our hair. The rest of the wetness would just have to wait until we could change at the motel. We went into the restaurant for mugs of hot chocolate to diminish the chill that racked our bones.

•. •. •. •. •.

The public address system boomed above the chatter in the restaurant, "Lift riders parked at the foot of Sandia Peak prepare to depart now. A substantial storm is moving toward us. Do not delay. Come to the platform now. You must leave now! We have rain gear for you."

The voice insisted. Urgent, intense in its message.

•. •. •. •. •.

Hot chocolate be darned. We bolted from our chairs and hurried onto the platform. We were not the first riders in line, but we were close enough to know we would be on our way down the mountain soon. We donned the rain gear for warmth, not for protection from the rain. We still were chilled from our last rain event. Hopefully, we would be in the parking lot and gone before the rain arrived.

Daylight dimmed, the wind swelled. We anxiously awaited the chair. The staff carefully loaded every other chair so that the downhill trip would be smooth, consistent, and quicker. Staff directed us to the footprints and a chair scooped us up. The bump on our legs was so welcome. We swung forward and the chair dipped over the front of the platform, into space. Miles of vast open terrain that spread out before us.

"Oh, no!" I stiffened. As I looked across the miles and miles of real estate before me, my fear of heights washed over me. The fear was drawing me into the space. I wanted to leap into the void. I didn't ask my friend to sing. I had heard her before, and I would rather just close my eyes and create other images. Better yet, I could watch the bike riders riding full-tilt downhill to beat the storm.

Below the descending chairs, a half dozen bike riders raced downward, leaping over obstacles, quickly divining the fastest pathway among the rocks and fallen branches. I focused my attention on those racers and prayed that we all would reach the parking lot before the storm reached us.

We did. Just. As my friend and I entered the car, the rain began. Before we could drive far, the rain became a torrent. The water rushed down the mountainside like a flashflood in a riverbed. Thankfully, we were able to pull off the roadway and wait for the storm to pass. We were must grateful that were not hanging in open space, partway down the mountain.

The Paddlers did not Linger
at the Lodge

Linger Lodge was mentioned in a conversation among friends the other day. An image of the rustic fishing camp popped into my mind. I was there only once, in the late 70s, but the place left an indelible vision in my brain for two reasons. First was the place itself. Linger Lodge, a legendary fishing camp out on Linger Lodge Road, off State Road 70, was, at that time, a collection of quaint cabins, an expanse of greenery next to the slow-moving Braden River, and an equally rustic wood-frame eatery. The second was the moment of bravado-gone-wrong between a couple of canoers, which is the basis of this story

The year is 1977. The main event here is the annual picnic for *The Bradenton Herald*. I had recently joined the company as its City Editor, which means I was responsible for the work of the reporters. Jerry Hill, *The Herald's* teller of its weekly outdoor tales and daily fishing forecasts, was in charge of this picnic—cooking and all.

Jerry also was the welcoming committee for my family and me. First, he introduced us to *the* Linger Lodge. Wow! I must say, none of my years of farming and tent camping among the creepy crawlies in the Midwest had prepared me for this. A collection of snake skins —very large snake skins—of several kinds hung on the walls in big dining hall. The girth of a couple of these skins was surely big enough to conceal small children.

Fortunately, our group was eating out on the picnic grounds, close to the river. There, we employees were treated to a meal of wild hog, a mixture of swamp cabbage and potatoes, seasoned well with bacon grease, and hush puppies. Those dishes were as different for me as the lengthy and fat snake skins on the wall. This Florida newbie put her trust in the genial cook whose size attested to his love of cooking and eating. These strange foods were surprisingly delicious. I even went back for an extra spoonful of the super tasty swamp cabbage.

What I really remember, however, was the impromptu entertainment that came later.

An assortment of games had been arranged, though I cannot recall the particulars. We also could rent one of Linger Lodge's canoes, which two of our sports writers, Gary and Jim, did. After lunch, an employee of the Lodge brought a forest-green canoe, about 12 feet long, along next to the wooden dock and held it steady for them.

Now, you need to know about these sports guys. Gary was average height, blond, strong-looking and walked with the appropriate jock swagger. I had worked at *The Herald* long enough to know that, although he was not the editor, he ruled the peons. Skinny, gangly Jim, on the other hand, was not in charge of anything, not even himself.

The two walked to the end of the dock, and Gary took the line from the Longer Lodge worker. Then the fun began.

The two seated themselves in the canoe. They adjusted in their seats and picked up the paddles. Gary pushed away from the dock. Jim gave a strong stroke as did Gary. Nothing happened. Each gave stronger strokes in succession, totally determined. Their only movement was with the current.

Someone in the picnic crowd began to laugh. The dudes turned their attention to the shore and then back to themselves. Gary the Dominate was seated looking over the downriver-pointing end of the canoe. Jim, the skinny, dark-haired, timid kid, was looking over the upriver-pointing end. Obviously, they had not discussed a paddling strategy or travel direction.

Gary snarled some obscenity, out of our earshot, at Jim, and they both stood up and harrumphed themselves around in the canoe, trying not to upend it as they did. Neither paid attention to the other. Each muttered some blue-tinged phrases into the afternoon air. Once again, neither took notice of or spoke a civil word to the other. It appeared that macho Gary believed that timid Jim would just know enough to let Gary the Diminate take lead in this debacle.

Ah, me. You can probably picture what happened next.

Gary was now facing upriver, Jim downriver. Not until they both were seated did either realize that were facing each other. They were drifting aimlessly in the river.

The two had captured the picnickers' total attention. The snickering gave over to outright laughter and jeering. Some of the younger men shouted directions at the two wise guys, who always let the newsroom folks know that, as sports guys, they were just too cool for words. The newsroom folks absolutely relished this stellar moment in the history of *The Bradenton Herald*.

Tempers had begun to rise in the canoe, however. Finally, Gary shouted "Sit still, you dumb f---!"

Jim being Jim did as he was told. An angry Gary stood and flounced around in the wobbling canoe until he was looking over the downriver end of the canoe. His behavior threatened to overturn the canoe that was floating free from the dock.

Petulantly, Gary plopped down. The crowd was really into the farce now, guffawing loudly and catcalling. This rowdy behavior achieved its goal. Gary, who believed that he was well above the behavior of mere news mortals, was so rattled he could barely reach the paddle behind him.

Flummoxed, nerves on edge, the men jammed their paddles into the river, Gary to the right, Jim to the left. Within seconds, the canoe shot downriver like it was motor driven.

The afternoon sun slipped behind the trees. The picnickers said their goodbyes and drifted toward their cars. We did, of course, wonder about the paddlers.

Most of the picnickers were gone from Linger Lodge. I don't recall whether anyone hung around for the men.

Gary and Jim may have avoided further ridicule that night, but they had escaped nothing. Fresh waves of laughter and teasing awaited them the next day in the newsroom.

The headline pinned to the bulletin board didn't help.

Canoe Trip Flummoxes Sports Writers
Which Way Did They Go?

The Tuxedo Junction

The names and places have been changed to protect the foolish.

Round 1—April 1978

"Excuse me, Chad." The tall, broad-shouldered man with boyish blond hair looked too young for his title and too big for his desk. Chad was a sizeable, distinguished man in his 50s whose footprint of influence in the community was equally imposing, if not intimidating. It was best if one approached him in a respectful, not familiar, manner. "Do you have a minute?"

"Hey, Shirley. Come on in." He seemed congenial at the moment.

Chad Lewis is publisher of *The Register Tribune*. I am standing on the threshold of his office. In my hand is the memo about the newly announced "The Register Tribune Tribute." The event promised to honor the academic achievements and community contributions of select county high-school seniors. Great idea, but the tenor of the memo has plucked my feminist nerve, and, now, I am about to twang Chad's sexist string.

"This program promises to be an exceptional contribution to our community. Particularly in its formal recognition of our high-school seniors." I say, as I waggle the memo in my hand. Tuxes and gowns needed all around, the memo says.

"I think you're right about that, Shirley." The tone of his reply indicated that he believed a "but" was coming.

"Chad, I noticed something that probably was an oversight, but I want to be sure. It says that *The Register* is going to pay for the rental of the tuxes. Will there be an equal stipend for the women to put toward their gowns?"

"No." He said. No hesitation. No reservation. Just a dispassionate, firm "No."

"May I know why the disparity?"

He settled casually, legs crossed, into his high-backed black-leather chair. "Women have gowns, men don't have tuxes," he said, his gaze unswerving.

His reply nettled my composure, and I did my best to stifle the rising prickle.

"Well, okay, Chad," I said, the nettles raking across my resolve. "But I can tell you for sure that the young women in the newsroom are not socialites and certainly cannot afford ball gowns on what we pay them. And the only gown I have is my nightgown. Thank you for your time, Chad." I held my irritation/anger the best I could and returned to the newsroom.

In full disclosure, the women in the newsroom had not asked for my intercession. I took the initiative because I believe in fairness, and because, as City Editor, I saw myself as their informal leader. I was, after all, the only female in a position of authority of any kind. I was a single mother to five children and a ball gown was an expensive proposition for me, too.

The female reporters were young, just out of college, and they certainly were scrimping to make ends meet and to have some fun on the pittance *The Register Tribune* was paying them. Most important to me was the cost of their obligation. Any woman who was asked to participate in this formal affair was obliged to accept. Hence, my displeasure with the disparity in the company's financial support. Displeasure? Heck. I was downright snarky about it.

The event was designed to honor, with significant pomp and circumstance, qualified high-school seniors for their involvement to the community, as well as for their academic superiority. The students qualified through written answers to a page of questions and interviews with persons from the business and nonprofit communities.

I report here that the program was outstanding, beautifully staged and carried out. The honored seniors beamed as they walked onto the stage, with an orchestral assist, to take their special seats under the bright lights. When the festivities ended, the award winners were ecstatic and hugged everyone within reaching distance. In the community, rings of pride and enthusiasm rippled for days, and *The Register Tribune*, for the short term anyway, stopped being "bottom cover for the bird cage."

Dare I say, too, that the publisher lapped up the praise.

Round Two—April 1979

Again, the memo was absent any mention of a stipend for the women to put toward their gowns. Chad sang the same song, second verse: Women have gowns, men don't have tuxedos. Inasmuch as the publisher was the final word on all things financial, the request died an unceremonious death, under yet another flat "No."

This time, the women had asked for my help. The new hires were offended by the expensive obligation. Evening gowns were a burdensome expense, and, of course, wearing last year's gown was not a possibility. Additionally, rent-a-gown shops were not yet in vogue.

Chad knew that the women had asked me to intervene, and he reminded me that I was technically part of management. Nevertheless, injustice snaps my backbone firmly into place. So, again, I asked, humbly, for parity. It was another futile request.

The second year was as successful as the first. "The Register Tribune Tribute Awards" succeeded in stirring excitement in the community. The audience and the participants milled about in foyer, buoyed by the images and the feeling of the night's joyful triumph.

Round Three—April 1980

This year, I knew better than to subject myself to even momentary futility. Chad was a well-heeled man, longtime king-of-the-hill in the Oakley Country Club set. In his experience, women did what their men told them. I was not one of his women, however.

The reporters and page-assembly women who reported to me hoped for positive information about the battle for fairness. I said only that this may be the last year for the inequity. They looked confused. "Trust me." I replied to their questioning eyes.

At my desk, I checked the memo for the fitting schedule for tuxedos. Fittings would begin in two weeks.

I arrived at the tuxedo shop at the earliest time and day available. I knew that the men would wait until the last minute, so I took advantage of their procrastination. At Ted's Tuxes, I got out of the car, squared my shoulders, and headed toward the door.

"I am with *The Register Tribune*," I said as the door closed behind me. "I am here to be fitted for a tux." I handed Ronald, the 20-something clerk, my newly printed "Managing Editor" business card, as evidence of my association with the newspaper. He looked askance. Maybe stunned would be a better word.

I stood a little taller, adopted my best don't-cross-me Mom look, and said, "I am quite serious, Ronald, and I expect your silence about this. If there is any question about the bill, I shall pay it." I tried for the imperious Bea Arthur (Maud of the Golden Girls) look. You know the one in which her attitude and great eyebrow move frosts everyone in the immediate vicinity. A friend once told me that when I was out of my element, as I certainly was then, just do theater. On this day and at this moment, I was Oscar ready.

As I left the tux shop, I turned and said, "I remind you that you are to say nothing. Not to your employer or to the any of the men from *The Register Tribune*." I even gave him the "Mom eyebrow" to emphasize my seriousness.

Well, it is safe to say I turned heads when I exited our car at the ceremony at the Municipal Auditorium. I looked smashing in my sassy hairdo and tuxedo. The ordinary, even dull, me had turned flamboyant. The crowd waiting in the foyer watched aghast as I stood at the car door and pulled myself together, gathering a modicum of courage to go through with this part of the theater role.

Backstage, the women were wide eyed. The men from the composing room, the place where we piece together the pieces of the puzzle that would become the morning's edition of *The Register Tribune,* gave me a thumb's up. They knew about the money contest. When I stepped from behind the stage curtains to make my presentation, I heard the collective intake of air from the audience

Although tuxedos for women were, in fact, the rage in *Women's Wear Daily,* the authority on women's fashion in New York, Manatee County folks are not fond of such an unabashed difference. Even with the floor-length velveteen skirt below the tuxedo jacket, very white shirt, cummerbund, and black tie, I was still way too different for them that night. Furthermore, I did not like being in the spotlight. This was, however, the time to take a stand.

The tuxedo became the junction between the way it was and the way it would be: fairness for the women.

Would it surprise you to learn that the women participating in the 1981 version of the awards ceremony received an amount equal to the rental of tuxedos? I am unsure whether the publisher worried more about what I would do next or the possibility that all of "his women" might show up in tuxes.

Surfing Backward

As I surfed the channels the other night, I stopped on Turner Classic Movies, which was showing *The Great Broadcast of 1937*. George Burns and Gracie Allen were just entering the storyline to pitch their act to the head of a failing radio station. The ratings of the station were very low (Ratings concerns in 1937? Seriously? You mean ABC, NBC, and CBS have competed in a ratings war for nearly a century?)

I credit George and Gracie, with her quirky twist of words and their meaning, with unleashing my love of playing with words when I was in grade school. Their conversations, which were both nonsensical yet strangely reasonable, piqued my imagination.

Nevertheless, as much as I liked George and Gracie's shtick, the audio sound of that era was harsh, the picture flat, and the actor's actions exaggerated. I wanted to watch the movie, because it was filled with other acts, like Bob Hope, Jack Benny, Martha Raye, Bing Crosby, and others, who had become part of my history, but the mechanics of the production irritated me. I left the room. I went into my office, which is around the corner from the living room. I could still hear the sound of the dialog. With the wall between the television and me, the dialog sounded more intimate, like the voices of old on the radio.

As I swiveled back and forth in my leather office chair, the old sound carried me on a journey through my memory machine. Instead of watching a movie about radio broadcasts, I was drawn to a distant yesterday, when radio and imagination were our only outside entertainment.

For instance, I recalled Grandpa Kent, my mother's father, hunched over on a straight-backed chair in front of their shiny-oak floor-model RCA radio. Its bright-green cat's eye narrowed as Grandpa carefully adjusted the signal for clarity.

Grandpa always looked the same: the sleeves on his blue work shirt rolled to the elbows that were leaning on the twill thighs of his grey work pants. Generally, he was listening to the revered broadcaster, Harry Heilmann, announce games for the Detroit Tigers baseball team. (Heilmann also had distinguished himself as a first baseman for the Tigers.) In fall and winter, Grandpa assumed the same positions for broadcasts of the Detroit Lions football team.

Grandpa Kent had never seen a Tigers' game or a live Lions' games in Briggs Stadium, more than 25 miles away. Still, he could see it all through the experiences of the announcer, which were reinforced by the stories and the photographs in the *Detroit News*. He picked up a copy of the newspaper every morning, on his way to work in the auto-parts factory. Hoot Evers, George Kell, Hal Newhouser, and Fred Hutchinson, all standouts for the Tigers, were real guys to Grandpa.

Then my thoughts drifted to Grandma Kent, who never listened to sports or any "Nonsense like that." I suspect, however, that Heilmann's voice settled in as she rocked way in her massive oak rocker with the arms that curled around and under themselves while she crocheted or knitted. She preferred to listen to Karl Haas and his *Adventures in Good Music*. Haas made his wonderful classical music understandable for us simple folks. (Forty years later, I interviewed Dr. Haas for the local newspaper. He was as gracious in person as he was on WJR in Detroit and then on WUSF/NPR in Tampa.)

Grandma also listened to the Hartz Mountain Canaries every Sunday afternoon. As a youngster, I never quite understood her fascination for birds singing to waltzes and Hawaiian music. They were just birds doing what they were born to do, chirp and twitter, only they were doing it for the prominent bird-food purveyor that sponsored the program. It also irritated me that they were not singing in rhythm to the music. I think Grandma never missed a single program. She listened to her singing birds over a small table-model radio, seated atop the asbestos covering on the radiator next to her chair, where she also kept a tub of popcorn.

Those pleasant memories dissolved into reverie about my own fascination with radio broadcasts. Late Sunday evenings, I listened to mysteries on the small, blue radio in my bedroom.

The evenings began with "Mr. Keen, Tracer of Lost Persons," which was sort of a forerunner of "Without a Trace" on television in later years. Mr. Keen was a kindly, older man who found missing persons, generally alive, but they sometimes were dead.

Mr. Keen was followed by "The Shadow," which began with a startling minor organ chord and the words, "Who knows what evil lurks in the hearts of men? The Shadow knows." This declaration was followed by a creepy, evil, "Wha, ha, ha, ha, ha . . ." laugh. The Shadow was really a man named Lamont Cranston who donned the cloak of invisibility to fight bad guys like The Black Master, Kings of Crime, The Five Chameleons, and The Red Menace.

By the time those two half-hour shows ended, the sun had set, and my room, save the yellow glow from the radio dial, lay in darkness. "The Green Hornet" buzzed in next, and as he did, I slid under the covers. "The Green Hornet" fought the really bad guys, and I just knew they were slinking about, waiting for my vigilance to wane.

The last half hour opened with the sinister sounding squeak of the door to "The Inner Sanctum." This program was full of really evil people and murderers and other assorted bad guys who were so scary that I pulled the covers up under my nose. Sometimes these guys were so bad, and gunshots popped through the darkness so loudly, that I pulled the covers over my head. Occasionally, I would lift the corner so some air could come in, but, mostly, I kept hidden until the door to the Inner Sanctum closed for the night.

A burst of loud laughter jolted aside the flat sounds of yesterday and drew my thoughts back to reality. George and Gracie were busy saving the radio station with their zany repartee, and I felt sad that children don't have the opportunity to know how vital their imaginations are. A good imagination is cheaper and bigger and better than any drug, and you carry its potential with you always. I believe imagination exceeds technology. As a matter of fact, without the imagination of very bright visionaries there would be no technology, no wild crashing and banging and super agile characters who never get shot.

Nevertheless, in my childhood, the characters and the scenes were only as bad or as ugly as my imagination made them. The sounds may have been supplied, but the degree of fierceness, the evilness were up to me. I preferred to create, maybe even delighted in creating, my own pictures of destruction and gore. Mine were softer around the edges.

Riding the Rapids

This is one of the messages I sent home on my vacations. I traveled alone, and my children wanted some assurance that I was reasonably okay. Sometimes, the messages were "after-the-fact" positive missives. I never called home. I did not want anyone to try to dissuade me from whatever adventure was on my agenda.

July 11, 2012

Well, family, today, I learned the true, humbling meaning of "wringing wet" in one of my most exciting and exhausting experiences yet. I'll tell you about it right after I take a nap. Everything in my body is pulling me toward bed. And it's only 6 o'clock.

July 12, 2012

Sorry. My nap became a full night's sleep, in my clothes, which is good. Now, I have a clear mind and the wit to write about my extraordinary rafting trip yesterday on the Nantahala River Gorge.

I know that none of you were aware that I might come whitewater rafting on my vacation, but that's your Mom. I can't recall if I even mentioned that I was coming to NC, but I am here. Story follows.

Picture this: Dozens of tourists mingling on a massive platform, loosely queued to load into the open train cars that will take us from Bryson City, NC to Fontana, more than an hour away. We rafting people will disembark in Fontana for our adventure.

Rain continued to fall steadily, umbrellas popped up. A man asked if I wanted to share his huge golf umbrella. I declined. I smiled and said, "Thank you, but, no. I'm going whitewater rafting today, and wet is wet." He laughed and wished me well.

The train arrived, and the crowd crowded. The crowding always surprises me. We don't have to fight for a seat. The company sells only as many tickets as they have seats. And all of the seats are the same: wooden, no padding, and open air. Craziness.

This was not an ordinary ride. For one thing, I could see the Nantahala River, with all of its rapids and rocks, and some rafters already on their trip. I smiled. I was really going to do this thing. The lady next to me said her 73-year-old sister was thinking about whitewater rafting, but she was afraid for her. "I'm 74, and I know my kids are fretful about my escapades.

But they'll have to get over it. Who knows how long I have left? Like the song says, 'I'm gonna live 'til I die.'" She chuckled, and we click-clacked up the mountain.

(In truth, kids, I am living this experience in thanksgiving and joy. When I attended the John C. Campbell Folk School in 2007, between chemo treatments, I made a promise to me. If I survived the five-year window after chemotherapy for my third cancer, I would celebrate with a whitewater rafting trip, an easy one, but rafting for sure. As you know, I passed that milestone last August, and I am celebrating.)

The train swayed over tracks that were laid in the days of the Tennessee Valley Authority's construction of dams, back in World War II. Below us, in the depths of the lake behind Fontana Dam, lay hundreds of homes sacrificed to the dam and the water supply for the greater area.

The train rocks along, swaying with the imperfections in the aged track line. Swaying is one thing, rocking about 15 to 20 degrees from side to side is quite another—especially when one needs to use the facilities. Well, I think you don't need much of a description to see the degree of difficulty in this feat of balance and decorum. From my perspective, this was not swaying to the music; it was more like rock around the clock.

When we arrived at the outpost in Fontana, the passengers staying aboard for the roundtrip waved goodbye as we rafters disembarked. It reminded me of the ballroom scene in *The Sound of Music*, where everyone waves to the children on their way to bed. No one sang "goodbye" to us, however.

The sun had shone throughout our ride up the mountain and to the river; now, a steady stream of rain drizzled as we walked to the ghastly green school bus, our transportation to the launch site. The weather was just as wet five miles later.

Brilliant-blue rafts sat in the parking lot, with a collection of splash jackets, personal flotation devices (PFD), and paddles, loaded inside. The jackets were provided to help us retain body heat, not to keep us dry on our excursion. (They were way late on the dry part, anyway.)

We pulled on the jackets, as Pappy, a man in his 60s, balanced himself on a raft's outer ring, instructed us in fitting the PFDs. Pappy was a mountain man for sure. A well-weathered Tilley hat sat above his ruddy, white-bearded face. His scruffy denim shirt and his faded jeans, frayed at the pockets, completed the look.

Pappy finished his instructions and warnings, the rain continued.

Rick, the guide for our raft, fitted our PFDs to us. While he tugged at straps and checked buckles, Pappy warned us in a dire tone of voice: "Do not! Do not loosen your PFD in any manner! They are to stay snug against your body. This is to ensure your safety.

"If you should have an out-of-boat experience, someone will be able to grab your PFD straps and pull you to safety. If you adjust your PFD to be comfortable, instead of snug, you could slip through your device and . . . well, you figure it out."

I listened to Pappy's instructions and watched the crowd of rafters mill about—and whine. Oh, my. What a group of tenderfeet, or maybe it's greenhorns. Whatever one calls them, they're not going to have a good day.

We Country Mice understood that this was going to be a cold, wet day. We had listened to the weather report, and we were prepared for the inclement day ahead with shoes, pants, hats, and long-sleeved shirts. The City Mice, however, especially their children, hugged themselves and whined through chattering teeth. "It's so cold." "How long is it going to rain?" "Do we have to wear that ugly blue thing (PFD)?" Those children were so accustomed to comfort, they were, to me, certified wussy butts. They shivered in flip-flops, tank tops and short shorts. Did they think they were at

Disney World in warm Florida? Whatever were their parents thinking? I shook my head to clear my brain of the nonsense and the stark awareness that these malcontents were assigned to my raft.

Once we were appropriately attired, Pappy schooled us in what to do if we should happen to find ourselves in an unfortunate "out-of-boat experience." "Well," his soft North Carolina drawl wrapped itself around the warning. "You won't have one of those if you wedge your outside foot under the seat in front of you. With your foot wedged, you will not have an out-of-boat experience." Pappy emphasized his message with that stern, ominous look that said, "I'll be watching you."

Each crew was obliged to carry its raft down a wooded trail to a sheltered area of the Nantahala. Rick told us that we would be rafting on easy rapids. Maybe a two on a scale of One (totally wussy) to Five (for the young, fit, and adventurous). Nevertheless, rafting— safe rafting—requires attention to instructions and information.

"If you fall out of the raft, do not seek the tree roots along the river for safety," Rick warned us. "The water action around them will pull you under." Then he delivered the paddling protocol.

"I will direct you in specific situations. Sometimes, you will 'pull,' in a normal forward stroke. Sometimes you will 'push,' like you are trying to force the raft backward. Sometimes, I will tell one side to push, the other side to pull. You provide the steering. Just be ready to do what I say when I say it.

"Let's practice. Everyone, pull! Right side: pull two, left side: push two!" The raft skewed to the right. "Right: push—hard, hard!" The raft skewed the other way. "Left: pull—hard, hard!" The raft came back in line with our direction of travel. "Great! Now, let's have some fun," Nick said, as he settled onto the raft, paddle in hand. Rick did a lot of directing to avoid rocks and to keep us in the best navigational path possible.

Well, through the hours in the rain, the fog and the rapids, I avoided the out-of-boat experience. Instead, I had three in-the-boat experiences. I was seated on the rear of the raft's donut, not in the raft as the others were. When we hit waves and rocks at the same time, I slipped downward into a space the size of a galvanized washtub in the bottom of the raft. Given my size and the size of the tub, this event was the equivalent of docking the Queen Mary2 in a teacup. Falling into this wedged position was easy; getting out and back onto the donut required the determination of our strapping young guide and the bulk of Jim, the guy in front of me, to provide enough heft to hoist the QM2 back into position. The second time, I had a workable plan to haul myself out. It was not easy, but I managed.

When we crashed over the falls at the end of our trip, the bump dropped me into the tub for the last time. The raft stopped moving. What a relief. However, the folly of my youthful thinking lay bare before me. About three hours and eight miles ago, I was full of energy and eager for the challenge. Now, I was wringing wet from being awash in 50-degree water and continually rained upon, and bulked up with a wet PFD. I felt a lot older than when we began.

The City Mice clamored out of the watercraft in search of warmth. I did not clamor. I was the last to leave the raft. My legs were wobbly, and my knees did not want to help me. With great difficulty, I got into a position where I could get one knee on the retaining wall, when two strong arms took mine and pulled me ashore. It would have helped if Rick, the guide, had given my stern a shove, but he was too gentlemanly for that. When I stood upright, I nearly fell backward into the water because my knee wanted to give out. Oh, no. That was not going to happen. I forced my body way forward, toward the hill.

Jim, the big fellow who had sat on my foot throughout our trip, was carrying three paddles, as he passed me. "Let me take one of those for you, Jim,"

I said, and literally grabbed a paddle from his hand. I was not being nice. I needed that paddle to steady me up the four concrete steps to solid ground.

My endurance trial was not yet over, however.

I trudged down the dirt road toward the ghastly green bus, one slow step after another. My drenched scrubs dragged on my thighs with each step. I was exhilarated, but I also was exhausted. Staying focused enough to not have an out-of-boat experience, expending great physical effort paddling vigorously with or against the current to keep the raft properly positioned, responding to the guide's insistent, frequently forceful directions. . . I was purely worn out.

Still wearing the bulky, restrictive PFD, I used the paddle as support. Step by slow step, I drag myself toward Wildwater's ghastly green school bus.

"Oh, Lord," I think, as I look at the stairwell in front of me. I have conquered a portion of the Nantahala in rain, fog, and over rapids. Now, now in my acute exhaustion, I must scale a mountain.

Have you seen the steps on a school bus recently? Gazelles and young humans, definitely not pleasingly plump older women, scale these three metal steps to safety and comfort. I grabbed the railing to my left, pushed myself up, onto the first of the stairs, with the paddle. I bumped against the dashboard and then back into the safety barrier on my left, where the railing is.

Finally, I gained purchase on the floor of the bus. I felt like one of the rainbow characters in the Jimmy Dean breakfast commercial. If I could just have one of his sausage sandwiches, the sun would shine all around, and I would suddenly be as light as air and perky. Then, I surely could make it to my seat, smiling, happy, revived. Hope springs eternal.

I shrugged out of my PFD before I sat down. Now it dripped on me, but I could move more freely. The paddle stood between my knees. The driver came down the aisle to count passengers. Satisfied he had everyone, our journey to lunch began. It felt grand to sit quietly.

When we reached the outpost, I waited for the younger, eager and still mobile rafters to exit before me. Then, I willed my body to stand. I gripped my paddle, my PFD, and my large bag of dry clothes and shoes. The doorway was just as cramped and forbidding on the way out as it was on the way in, just easier going down. I threw the equipment onto the ground and lowered myself down the mountain. I gathered the paddle and the PFD and carried them 30 feet or so to the outpost shed. We deposited the PFDs in a tub of water and the paddles into the hands of a guide who directed us to the changing stations.

Ah, the changing stations. Another challenge in endurance. Each was slightly more constrictive than I had imagined they might be. Mine measured about two-feet deep and four-feet across, with a cloth privacy curtain hanging from an overhead rod. A 12-year-old could manage well in these confines. As could an anorexic model, changing from one virtually nonexistent bathing suit into another. But we women who clean our plates at mealtime and wear shoes, socks, pants, and shirts to keep warm on the river, faced a significant test in this phone booth. A triangular-shaped wooden seat, about eight inches on each of its sides, was wedged into one corner.

I sat on the pretend seat and considered how to begin. Everything was so wet and sticky, and there was no real room to wrangle the shirt and pants off my wet, sticky body. I think changing my clothes may have been more daunting than the rafting. I dropped my water-soggy shoes and my drenched clothes into the grocery bags I brought with me. I piled the squishy bags into my tote. Then, I dried with the towel I borrowed from the motel, pulled on dry clothes. I gave up trying to drag socks on over damp feet. I just jammed my damp bare feet into my shoes and headed for the food. The rain continued, so I wrapped the towel around my shoulders, not that wrapping a damp towel around my shoulders made any sense at all.

"Where is the food?" I asked of a fellow rafter. He pointed toward the top of the hill. I could hear laughter and talking from the shelter among the trees on the top of the hill. I could smell barbecue from the shelter among the trees on the top of the hill where people were laughing and talking. Thirty-two wide wooden steps separated me from the people and the food in the shelter among the trees on the top of the hill.

And I thought the bus steps had been intimidating.

This climb was Mt. Everest relocated to North Carolina to punish me, I supposed, for my hubris in thinking I was equal to the rigors of whitewater rafting. I have no idea how long it took to climb those 32 steps, but it felt like a freaking eternity. My thighs throbbed. My breathing was labored.

When I arrived at the food, I wobbled to a seat at the nearest picnic table. April, one of the perky young guides, asked if I wanted sweet tea or lemonade. She had to be kidding. I couldn't reply. I sat there, puffing like the steam engine that pulled us up the mountain and stared at her. A light of awareness shone in her eyes. "How about if I get you some water?" I nodded and smiled, weakly.

Once I could breathe again, I fixed a plate of barbecue, coleslaw, and baked beans and sat down to enjoy it. The coleslaw was my favorite kind: just chopped vegetables, without a sloppy mixture of mayonnaise and whatever they mix with it. In eager anticipation of the taste, I scooped a pile onto my fork. As I raised the fork toward my mouth, my hand went into spasm. The affliction spontaneously shared my slaw with my tablemates. Flakes of chopped cabbage and carrots drifted down upon them like a curious snowfall in July. After that, eating my slaw and my beans was a two-handed job, like a child just learning to drink from a cup.

The rest of the afternoon and evening was the proverbial blur. Finding my way back to my motel eluded me for a bit. I cruised Bryson City, looking for the way north to Cherokee. After a couple of meandering circuits through town, I saw the route sign. It felt so good to be sitting on a soft seat that I didn't mind the extra driving.

Back in Cherokee, I parked my Relay in front on the Hampton Inn and just sat there. I pushed its door open. I could not move voluntarily. I grabbed my left pant leg and lifted my leg toward the doorway. I twisted a little to the left with my leg. Then I dragged my right leg around to the doorway. I slid off the seat, down to the parking lot. For a moment, I considered leaving my bag of wet clothes where it was, but thought better of the idea. When I got to my room, I dropped the bag in the bathroom sink and lay down on my bed with my clothes on. I had not the energy to twist a wet sock. Morning would be soon enough for that.

I have had quite enough for this day.

Gargle? With Lidocaine?

You probably have heard the phrase, "The cure was worse than the illness." Well, I recently experienced that adage firsthand.

In the night, I had begun to develop a sore throat. My sinuses, a chronic problem in my life, were draining and irritating my throat, big time. By morning, swallowing was a serious problem, and the day ahead promised to be full of pain and suffering. I rolled over and sat up on the side of my bed.

To shower or not to shower? I wondered as I sat and worked the kinks from my muscles. I knew I would head to the walk-in clinic before I did anything else. The clinic opens at 7 a.m. The time was 6:10 a.m. Was I going with a quick tidying or fully refreshed? Refreshed was the only answer. Growing up, the family rule was, "There never is a good excuse for leaving the house looking as disheveled and miserable as your body feels." As a kid, that axiom ranked right up there with another winner in a long list of them: Never leave the house wearing dirty underwear. You might be in an accident.

What did the one have to do with the other, my little brain had wondered those many years ago.

The logic in these axioms escaped me then, and it does now, but those absurd phrases stick with you over the years. No matter if they are basically dumb.

Anyway, I showered and dressed and drove off to the clinic, a mile or so away. Surprisingly, the intake room was not busy. Generally, the waiting room is full, nearly as soon as the place opens. Today, however, I had just enough time to complete the requisite paperwork before I was called to an examining room. I waited a little longer for the doctor, who at end of his silence and a hmm or two, he declared, "It appears that you are on your way to a sinus infection." Nothing new there. That had been my thought as I sat on the side of my bed. "Your sore throat is from your sinus drainage."

He ordered prescriptions for a nasal spray, an antibiotic, and something to gargle, which were sent to my pharmacy. I gave the pharmacy a couple of hours to pull together the order before I went to collect them.

"It will be a little while longer before we have the gargle solution ready," Linda, the pharmacy assistant, told me. "We have to compound it." Wow! This must be some mystical, magical stuff if they have to "compound" it. The gargle liquid would come from the pharmacy's equivalent of The Betty Crocker Cookbook.

All ingredients whipped together from scratch. I didn't care. I just needed something to soothe my throat. It hurt to drink water.

You know that phrase I mentioned at the beginning of this story? The one about the cure being worse than my sore throat? The truth was about to be manifest.

The directions on the gargle solution said: Swish, gargle and spit 15 to 30 ml every 1-2 hours for five days. Sounds simple enough, right? No, not so simple in practice.

To begin with, my quick computer conversion told me that 15 ml equals three teaspoons or one tablespoon. I would start there. A tablespoon isn't all that big.

Then, I looked at the ingredients. I was stunned. Think about this: The main ingredient in the solution is lidocaine. Yep. Lidocaine. The drug that numbs the gums before dental work. The local anesthetic injected before pulling a gaping laceration together with sutures. That lidocaine. Lidocaine numbs things. It renders the area totally without feeling. And I was supposed to gargle with it. Seriously?

I thought perhaps all of those learned medical people knew something that I did not. Like, maybe, saliva dilutes the potency of the anesthetic, or something. So, I poured the liquid into a tablespoon and dumped it into my mouth to quickly "swish and gargle." Well, I swished. And, of course, all tissue was immediately numbed. I tried to gargle.

My gargle was dead; my gag reflex, however, was alive and well. Fortunately, I was standing at my kitchen sink because the gag reflex spewed the pink liquid into my stainless-steel sink. Bleah!

I tried to clear my mouth, but all of my mouth is dead. Dead, I say! I can't swish water or anything. I'm coughing. Gagging. I'm sweating. Trying not to barf. (Who knew how that would turn out?) Splashing water on my face. Good grief! Had I offended the doctor? Was this some kind of practical joke? Did someone make a mistake with the pharmacy cookbook?

And I think the numbing stuff never made it to my sore throat.

Needless to say, I did not try this at home again. Not in "1-2 hours" or any other duration of time.

Instead, I resorted to my grandmother's tried-and-true remedy for nearly everything: a warm mixture of whiskey, a lot of honey, and a touch of lemon juice. Take often and follow with nap chasers. I also took a decongestant, which eliminated the drainage. Miraculously, within 24 hours, the whiskey, the honey, the nap, and the decongestant, made my sore throat just another memory.

The terror of the cure was quite remarkable and very memorable, however.

Germs

Bubble, bubble, toil and trouble.
Macbeth's witches brew a stew
in a cauldron not so subtle
as modern-day brewers do.

Present-day apothecaries scheme hard
to feed our fear of invisible microbes.
The germs, they declare, retard good
health, and create the germophobe.

Scrub, scrub and bubble the germicide
on your hands 'til you have sung
a verse of Old MacDonald to deride
thoughts of rinsing before your song is done.

An ugly fallacy lingers in this
money-making scheme in terms
of truth about this unhealthy risk
in our obsession to eradicate germs.

The dreaded bacteria are natural
inhabitants of every inch of skin,
our lungs, our intestines, our diurnal
and nocturnal functions. Every minute.

They live to protect us, these
fearsome creatures we cannot see.
They are the pit bulls that seize
with pride our germy enemies.

So, pitch the pretty pump bottles.
Let your germs continue to be
the fierce, invisible protectors that throttle
the real threat to glowing health and glee.

Hokey Pokey in the Tub

My first morning, a Thursday morning in December more than a dozen years ago, at Silver River State Park, began with a bang.

A bang. A bump, bump, bump, wham, whump, thump, and then— silence. This was followed with a tentative, fearful, "Mom? Are you okay?" My daughter called through the pocket door to the bathroom.

I had fallen in a very slippery shower/tub.

I had put my left foot in, and suddenly I was doing the Hokey Pokey, shaking all about, in the bottom of the tub. When the thunder of the moment ended, I lay there, the fine spray from the shower pelting my face, afraid to move.

Was I okay? "I'm not sure," I called back, turning my face away from the spray. "But I'm going to need your help." At that moment, I was too rattled to be embarrassed about lying naked in a heap in the bottom of the bathtub.

Sharon, my daughter, hurried in and turned off the shower. I tried to pull myself to a sitting position. "Just quit moving until we sort things out," she said. She sounded like I had over the years in any of the many spontaneous crises with my five children: concerned, but firmly insistent and in charge.

"First, we'll take care of this," she said, as she shoved a washcloth under my nose, which was bleeding, and wiped the blood off my chest. (My first nosebleed ever. Wow!) She checked my head and extremities for cuts, scrapes and lumps. There were none. She helped me to sit up.

No broken bones. Not even my nose, though the bridge was tender to the touch. Everything checked out fine, except for my left pinky, which was very sprained and mighty painful. My knees had big, red spots on them where they had banged against the tub and the hardware. My left shin was scraped, probably by the spigot at the end of the tub, where I lay crumpled at the end of my ride.

"Okay, you don't seem to be seriously hurt, so what do we do next?" Sharon asked.

"Well, I don't know what you are going to do, but I am going to sit right here and take a bath," I answered.

A bath! What a glorious idea! Baths in tubs had been out of the question in my stiffening years. So long as I was sitting here, however, I might as well make this a happy accident. At the very least, I could soothe my muscles in the hot water and regroup. "I'll let you know when I am ready to leave the land of slippery slopes."

Sharon, her husband Ron, and I were the advance guard for a Christmas holiday in the park. We had reserved three cabins for our family, the rest of whom—11 of them—would join us Friday night and Saturday morning. This day, we had been preparing for breakfast at Bob Evans, on State Road 40 in Ocala, and a trip to the grocery store for supplies. I usually start my day with a hot shower to waken my whole being. The slippery tub abruptly changed our plans.

I sat there, waiting for the water to rise around me, reflecting upon my wild ride. How long had the excitement lasted? Ten seconds? Thirty seconds? I remembered the first slippery step and thinking "Let go." Years in sports of all kinds had trained me to relax with a fall. My right leg was still on the outside of the tub, so I wasn't exactly a unit in motion, but I let the accident be a relatively safe one.

As I sat in the rising water, I squeezed hot water from the washcloth over my shoulders and down my back. I thought through my slip and fall. I remembered, but not in detail, the flailing of my arms and legs as inertia and the laws of physics held me in their grip. I remembered the incredible noise of my body slamming against the sides of the tub. I didn't recall hitting my face or the blow that accounted for my bloodied nose. I vividly remembered my relief when the noise and the pounding stopped. Still hearing the sounds of my fall, I soaped up and washed.

Bath over. It was time for the challenge: Getting out of this slippery hole. I called for Sharon.

"How are we going to do this?" She asked. She knew that I would have a plan.

"Very carefully," I said. "And with much thought."

All of the surfaces were way too slippery for me gain purchase for my exit, so our first challenge was to give me traction. I had thought about this. "First, wet a hand towel and lay it here, on the edge of the tub, then give me another towel, a hand towel will do, that I can lay in the bottom of the tub."

With those props, I was able to bring myself into a kneeling position. It was no small feat to both maneuver this old, uncooperative body in such a small space and kneel on a very rough towel with two very bruised knees. The alternative to my succeeding: calling in my son-in-law to help. Now, that was truly an incentive to get the job done. With Sharon's steady hand and strength, we were able to maneuver me into an upright position in the bathroom.

Our first stop on the road that morning was not breakfast at Bob Evans, but Walgreens, where I purchased a splint for my finger, some tape and some Tylenol. I had encased my hand in a bag of ice on our ride to Walgreens. Between the ice, the Tylenol and the stabilization of my finger, I enjoyed breakfast with little discomfort. My knees were a bit more bothersome, but, surprisingly, I had very little soreness in the rest of my body.

At the grocery store, Ron picked up a couple of packages of non-slip strips for the tub. The strips kept me upright in my morning showers. Nevertheless, I'm sure that the park service removed the strips after we left. To make sure that the cleaning folks knew that they hadn't been so tidy before we arrived, I left a note about the slippery tub and my accident on top of the newly installed strips.

As I write this account, early the next morning under the shade of an oak tree in the Big Scrub section of the Ocala National Forest, I am listening for the sound of the Polaris ATVs. I am waiting for Sharon and Ron to return from their ATV ride out on the plentiful trails in the forest. When they come back, I'll be taking my first ATV ride with one of them. Actually, I'll be driving one of the four-wheeled sport machines. Sore pinky and all.

Uncle Jim
and the Exasperating Hens

Today, I have passed through many small towns and acres of countryside in Georgia on my way to an even smaller town—Brasstown, NC. Brasstown is home to the John C. Campbell Folk School, one of the best folk-art schools in the southeastern United States. I am headed to JCC for a writing workshop with a published author.

As I drove through miles of very rural Georgia, I happened upon Aunt B's Bakery and Café, a surprise spot of life on U.S.76. The café is located on the enclosed front porch of an old, but neat, white house trimmed in green that sits back from the roadway on a little slope. Toward the back of the property, weathered farm equipment stands in front of some tired-looking buildings. The parking lot at Aunt B's is more like someone's side yard, with chipped stone spread around. Where and how I parked my vehicle was my choice; no white lines defined parking spaces.

The café had a half-dozen square tables covered in red-and-white checkered oilcloth crowded together.

The dining area was close enough to the kitchen that the cook could talk with customers through the big serving window.

For all its quaintness, Aunt B's served up a liberal corned-beef sandwich on delicious and fresh homemade white bread. This was accompanied by a generous portion of equally delicious and homemade potato salad and a frosty mug of strong tea. I was careful to specify "unsweetened" tea because Georgia sweet tea is way over the edge on sweetness for this Yankee.

Aunt B wasn't around this day. Uncle Jim was on duty. A polite man, was he. He had silver hair and beard, both close-cropped. His blue-and-white print suspenders set off his neatly pressed red-plaid shirt and sky-blue twill britches. As it turned out, Uncle Jim was an all-around colorful character.

While I ate my sandwich, he came out onto the porch to wipe the tables.

"I hear roosters up on the hill," I said. "Does that mean you raise the chickens that produce the brown, free-range eggs you sell?" I asked. A sign in the bakery case declared, "Free-range brown eggs, $1 a dozen."

Uncle Jim stopped, midstride, and turned a stern gaze in my direction. He pulled himself up straight and propped his hand and rag on his left hip. He leaned the other hand on the sideboard, next to the kitchen. He slowly shook his head and sighed in exasperation.

"No, Ma'am. I never raised chickens. Those danged hens belong to Allen," he said, "And I don't do business with him." Uncle Jim was getting cranky.

"Allen moved here about a dozen years ago with two roosters and eight hens. Within a year, there were chickens all over the place." Uncle Jim gestured wildly, his voice energized. "Frank, in the farm down the road, stopped countin' chickens running loose on his property at 80."

Uncle Jim stepped away from the window and emphasized his story with wild gestures. "And I tell you, Ma'am, I had more than a hundred of those danged birds runnin' around here! All told, there were about 300 chickens roaming everywhere.

"Allen came down here one day and told me we should do something about those wild chickens. He was all righteous like and thinkin' he was gonna get over on me.

"I said, 'Allen, those dang chickens aren't wild. They're yours!'

"'Naw, they ain't,' Jim,' he said to me, all innocent like. 'I brought two roosters and eight hens with me. Them's the only ones that are mine!'

"I told the damn fool he had a good bit to learn about chicken raising. Two roosters runnin' free and eight hens can make a powerful lot of chickens." Uncle Jim pounded his big fist the sideboard in disgust, as he recalled his conversation with Allen.

I was almost sorry I raised the subject. Almost sorry, I said, because his story was very entertaining.

Uncle Jim said he eventually called the folks at the county animal-control department. The animal-control put Allen on notice: Get rid of the chickens in this residential zone or pay some hefty fines. Uncle Jim didn't say how successful Allen was in his chicken round up, and I didn't ask.

But that wasn't the end of Uncle Jim's story. Mildred, a sturdy farm woman who lives a mile or so up the road, came to visit him one day. "Jim," she said, a warning tone in her voice, "I've got two broods of your chickens, and . . ."

"Stop right there, Mildred! Them ain't my chickens! They're Allen's! Go talk to him!"

I could see that the recounting of this episode was getting the best of Uncle Jim's restraint.

"'But I don't know him, Jim,'" she replied, flustered by his answer.

"Then call animal control! They ain't mine! And I'm not going to do a damn thing about 'em!" Uncle Jim got a little exercised right then and slammed his rag down onto my table.

I chuckled. "I suspect you did get things taken care of though."

"Yes, I did! But Allen and me, we don't talk anymore. And we sure as hell don't do business, either! Sorry, Ma'am." He flushed, as he apologized for the cuss words. "It's just a real sore subject here."

"Maybe you need to put up a sign that says, 'We sell brown, free-range eggs, but don't ask about the chickens.'"

He laughed and finished wiping the tables, as I wished him a blessed day.

I suspect that his story could have been a country yarn, but he was an amusing storyteller. You never know whether these mountain folks are telling the truth or just having fun with you. Either way, this unexpected respite put a smile in the rest of my trip.

Practice, Practice, Practice

A tourist on a street in New York City stopped an older man to ask, "How do you get to Carnegie Hall?" The man looked at the tourist intently and replied, "You practice, practice, practice!" The elderly man happened to be the legendary violin virtuoso Yehudi Menuhin. He was right, of course. I have no idea whether this story is factual, but it reminded me of my introduction to the rigors of music lessons many years ago. I was not thinking about Carnegie Hall, however.

I was in eighth grade at Novi Elementary School (MI), and I longed to play in the band at Northville High School, where I would be enrolled in the coming fall. The only thing I ever truly wanted in my short life was to play music.

Early in my years, I asked my Mother about getting a piano so that I could take piano lessons. "No!" She was emphatic. "You will lose interest, and then we'll have an expensive piece of furniture that will just take up room we don't have."

She might have had a point at the time. I was in elementary school, and elementary school-age children are known for their lack of focus.

Nevertheless, my little heart wanted to play music. I was so disappointed that the orange wax panpipe like candy whistled only one note, not many notes. I made a kazoo, but that was not satisfying. I wanted to play a real musical instrument. I really, really wanted to play real music. To no avail. My pleading lingered in the air like dust in the morning sunlight.

The years passed and so did the many classes of math and English and history. But no music, except, that is, for the dumb music classes. Everybody in class did the same thing, sang the same songs that sounded in the same sing-song way. Boring, boring, boring.

On Christmas break that year, I saw my friend, Kathy, then a freshman at Northville High. She told me about how great it was to be in the marching band. Marching band? The high school had a band? (I lived in the country, many miles from the high school, and had no knowledge of what happened there.) I peppered Kathy with question. How do you get to be in the band? What did she have to do to make that happen? She answered all of my questions. She even offered to have her dad pick me up on their way to band practice on Monday nights.

"How can I get into the band?" That was my most important question of all time.

"I didn't know that you play an instrument," she noted. Kathy played the alto saxophone. She had been taking lessons for a long time.

"I don't, but I will get one," I replied. I was so determined, so confident that I would, could accomplish my dream.

Then she spoke words of musical magic: "That's okay. They loan instruments to students. No charge." Oh, wow! If my mother thought she had dampened my musical spirit, she was wrong. So wrong.

Kathy and her dad did indeed stop for me each Monday night for the rest of the schoolyear. I was so excited that they would do that, that I waited on the roadside across from my house. They barely had to slow down for me to jump into the back seat of their Hudson. I was fascinated and ecstatic to watch the musicians and Mr. Lee, the director. He would tap on his music stand and the musicians stopped playing. He talked to them about one thing or another in the music, then, he would raise his arms, baton in hand. The musicians would bring their instruments to their mouths, and he started them playing with a downbeat of his baton. I learned about downbeats and other music language on the way home from practices.

I asked Kathy so many questions, and she answered them all on our trips home.

Along about February, as I approached graduation from elementary school, I began lobbying Mother to take me to see Mr. Lee. I explained that he was the director and would be the person to talk to about getting into the band. She resisted as relentlessly as I persisted. Finally, in April, she succumbed to my incessant nattering. I was so excited and determined that I actually called the school to see when Mr. Lee would be available. I made an appointment. That was a very bold move for this painfully shy 13-year-old. Mr. Lee agreed to meet me on the day after school closed for summer break in June.

On that important day, I wore my best skirt and blouse and felt really confident. Another first for me, that confidence thing.

Mr. Lee was a kindly gentleman. He never raised his voice at band practice, even when I thought he could have, should have to the boys who clowned around. Mr. Lee stood about my height (5'8"), was sort of portly, had graying hair that receded at the temples, and was neatly dressed in a grey suit, white shirt and grey striped tie.

He greeted me cordially and seated us at a small table in his small office. I was not at all nervous; way excited, but not nervous. I was fulfilling a life-long mission.

"So, Shirley, you think you want to play in the band." He stated his question.

"Yes, sir, I do." I replied and sat up straighter.

"What instrument do you play?"

"I don't play any instrument." He just looked at me. No expression.

"How do you think you can be in the band then?" His furrowed brows turned his face into a piercing question mark.

"My friend, Kathy, said that the school provides instruments, and that you provide lessons." More furrowed brows.

"Do you read music?"

"No, sir, but I am sure that I can learn." Now, raised brows.

At this point, I must say that, although I did not realize it at the time, I was one determined, if not shamelessly brazen, girl. What youngster would be so presumptuous as to believe that she could go from no music experience to ever becoming part of an established high school music program? It never occurred to me that I might not succeed in my unflinching belief.

Though I feel that Mr. Lee was a bit flummoxed, he did not openly challenge my plucky teenage behavior. He was too experienced for that. Instead, he got up and walked over to unlock a tall, metal cabinet. He removed a small black case and brought it over to our table. He popped the locks with his thumbs and opened the case to display a dinged-up, silver-colored metal clarinet. I expected to see a traditional black one. No matter, Mr. Lee was entrusting me with a real musical instrument. I didn't care what it looked like. I could hardly wait to hold it, which I did as he showed me how to put the reed on the mouthpiece and blow into it. He had me play each note on the scale to show me the fingerings that produced them. My insides quivered in my excitement.

In retrospect, I believe Mr. Lee was challenging me with the runt of the litter (the dinged-up metal clarinet), so to speak, to make good on my bravado. If I could rise above the challenge of the runt, then I had a chance to succeed.

With the clarinet, he also gave me my first book of simple music to practice. I was so ready to play music, to practice, practice, practice.

•. •. •. •. •.

I practiced every minute I could. My father disapproved of my need for music. To him, music was a waste. So, I practiced away from him. In the car in the driveway, with my music propped on the glove-box cover. In the garage, where I leaned my music on the massive, grubby vise. I practiced inside only when my father was away from the house. But I practiced. And I struggled with producing strong, clean notes. The B flat was the worst. The runt was not going to do me in, however.

I was blessed that my father was a journeyman tool maker. This title meant that he was important in his job and often was expected to work overtime. Overtime kept him away from home for many extra hours nearly every day.

His increased absence was really welcome as the weather grew colder and the music more intricate and difficult. Cold fingers are too stiff to quickly play a line of sixteenth notes or many measures of sixteenth and eighth notes. Add to this challenge, my unskilled brain struggling to will my fingers to master the music. Playing inside absolutely facilitated my learning and my proficiency. This was helpful, because Mr. Lee continued to give me more-advanced, faster music to practice. I didn't really notice so much; I just played.

When I went for my lesson just before Christmas break, Mr. Lee walked over to that tall, metal filling cabinet and removed a shiny black case, the size of the case I had. He placed it on the table where we had our first conversation and popped the locks. There in the plush blue-black velvet lay a shiny black clarinet. I was so overwhelmed that I couldn't say a word. I'm sure Mr. Lee noticed the tears in my eyes, however.

"You have earned this." He said without fanfare. "Come to band practice on the Monday when we return from the holiday break. You will be sitting third chair." This is the equivalent of being the low player on the clarinet pecking order. "I'll take the instrument you have now when we finish today's lesson." Mr. Lee was a man who spoke important words only. We walked over to the practice area and today's lesson.

From June to December, I had become a member of the Northville High School Band. By the end of my time in the band, I had earned a music scholarship to Wayne State University in Detroit.

A Dream Shattered

It was my senior year in high school, and I faced a heavy choice: go to college on a music scholarship, or do what I think would gain my father's love.

Because I was the only female in the family of four children and because my brothers were the apples of my father's eye, I refused the scholarship. Not because I fully understood the gravity of my choice but because the emotionality of it weighed more.

When I announced, excitedly, that the high-school band director had granted me a music scholarship to Wayne State University, about 20 miles away in Detroit, my father brutally burst the bubble of my going to college.

"You're not going to college," he said. "Girls are too stupid to go to college. It's your job to get married and have babies."

The message from that experience more than 60 years ago has reverberated across my decades. What resulted as I wrote about this experience in a recent writing class at a summer-school experience in North Carolina was: One, it is time to let go of what my father said. He, like all of us, was the product of his generation, his upbringing. I did get married and bore five wonderful children. They did not seem to make much difference to how my father responded, however; Two, I needed to grow a backbone. If, after all this time, I didn't believe in what I wanted, nobody would. Three, no one should allow the memory of an event so long past affect more than the 60 years that memory had tainted. The bile from that disappointment has risen one too many times, even though I eventually had achieved a college degree.

With this recitation of that event in my summer class, the final recitation of that influential event, I have set myself free.

My father finally is dead in every sense. As I said, I got married and gave birth to five terrific children. Later, I earned my BA, with high honors, in writing at Eckerd College when I was 75.

Yesterday is dead and gone, and I celebrate with great joy my joint accomplishments of having those babies and earning my college degree.

Success after 57 Years

The receptionist at the Renaissance Center completed her transaction with the woman in line before me, and I moved toward the counter. The receptionist, whose attitude was as tightly wound as her hair, ignored me. She knew I was there. She had given me a disdainful, raised eyebrow look over the previous customer's shoulder.

I had come to the Renaissance Center, the community's official senior center in Bradenton, FL, ready to sign up as an official senior. Age wise, I am a senior. Nevertheless, I had not felt like a senior until I survived chemotherapy for breast cancer.

Weeks earlier, I had completed a year of chemotherapy to wipe out the cancer that resulted in my second mastectomy. The treatments had gone well, but now my brain was muddled. Simple tasks the had been routine a year ago challenged me. This confusion frustrated me. To my way of thinking, I was seriously diminished. This possibility angered me. To this point, my life had been energizing, interesting, enjoyable. What will become of me now?

"You are experiencing confusion from your chemo treatments," my oncologist told me. He suggested I read new books, start a new hobby, make lists, and other suggestions common to overcoming brain diminishment in the elderly.

The "You are getting old. So, what?" kind of thinking for a brain that had served me so well for 68 years was unacceptable. Until chemotherapy, I could easily complete basic math computations in my head. At this point, however, I was unable to add even a column of simple numbers in my head. How frustrating and annoying.

"Lord, deliver me from being a mental vegetable for the rest of my life," I thought.

Thanks to the wonder of technology, I was able to easily research the possibility of a more satisfying solution to my brain drain. My research showed that with some "serious effort" I could improve my thought patterns, my ability to think objectively, and do it systematically, efficiently.

I must, according to the literature, challenge my brain to heal itself. The challenge would require more than solving the New York Times crossword puzzle and making reminder lists. Which is why I showed up at the Renaissance Center. The center's online literature said that Tai Chi was the most popular class among senior citizens. Perhaps memorizing the system of moves and concentrating to execute them gracefully would begin the healing process.

Th Renaissance Center clearly was not going to be an answer. The receptionist never acknowledged my presence in her space. I slapped the brochure onto the counter and walked out. "What now?" I wondered. I walked to my car, muttering about her rudeness and lack of respect. Again, I wondered, "Now what?" I started driving, thinking of possible alternatives to the failed plan. None came to mind. My wandering delivered me to the front parking lot at State College of Florida. "What the heck? Why am I here?" "Administration Building—Testing," the sign said, with an arrow pointing the way. "Testing for college classes? Seriously? And then, "Why not?" I had nothing else to do with my life, my time is my own. I returned the next day, during regular testing hours, and completed a couple of hours of basic testing in math and English. After 55 years out of school, I needed two remedial-math classes and English 101, which was required of all new students. If math, a difficult subject for me, didn't stir the regrowth of my synapses and dendrites, what topic might? English had been fun since my first class in elementary school. It was like a game with words. I completed the remedial college math and the mandatory English class. I was having fun, even in math, so I decided to keep on keepin' on. The next semester I took another math class, and classes in ethics and humanities. I earned an A in each of them. I was taking classes that interested me to facilitate brain growth and loving every minute of every class.

One day, as I walked cross the SCF campus, I realized that I was walking in the presence of opportunity and success. I smiled. The college degree that eluded me in 1957 was within my reach. I turned on my heel and headed for the counseling office. I wanted to know what I had to do to earn my AA degree. If I worked diligently, the counselor said, I could acquire that prize in 2011. Because I had amassed enough transferable credits from years of classes at Black Hawk College in Illinois, I had fewer classes to complete. As a mother of five children, I sought adult contact and mental stimulation. Because my husband taught math in night classes, I was able to take credit courses for free.

I asked the "Now what?" question of a friend at lunch one day. She suggested I enter the Program for Experienced Learners at Eckerd College in St. Petersburg, just across Tampa Bay. She had completed the PEL program and then earned her master's degree in Colorado. She said the PEL program was unique and daunting. She was spot on. PEL students could take no more than two courses per semester because each course met five-hours twice weekly, for eight weeks.

We "experienced learners" produced in eight weeks what the regular students, the young ones, did in 16. In my final semester, I had two literature classes. Two books a week, with interpretive essays expected for each of them. Yes, I read and wrote well into the nights. This snafu was an accident of class availability, not lack of planning. Nevertheless, when I submitted the final papers for that semester, I knew that I had climbed an academic mountain.

In reality, the whole college experience was daunting, yet exhilarating and joyful. I was the eldest in all of my classes—by about 25 years. This challenged me to rise above my stereotypical thinking—and theirs—about how "elders" should behave. I got over that nonsense soon enough. My advanced age changed the warp and the weft of the classes, gratified me that my experiences added valuable depth and texture to their learning. Moreover, the younger students introduced me to the finer points of "now," awareness of current thinking and attitudes.

On both graduation days, my family—five children, spouses or significant others, and my granddaughter—cheered and hooted loudly as I proudly walked across the stage and accepted my diploma from the president of each college.

My pride in accomplishment and satisfaction were doubled when I reminded myself that the journey toward a college degree that should have begun in 1956, when I was 18, ended 57 years later, at age 75. On May 12, 2013, I proudly held my BA in fine arts, magna cum laude, along with the college's coveted award for my writing portfolio.

Homework in the Rain

In rain or shine, in wind or heat
I write my precious words in the park.
Today, the rain is lazy.
The drops talk among the leaves

and send a multitude of gentle concentric circles
away from each wet bead that joins the many
in the small pond. A rhythmic, soft-shoe patter
glides down the metal roof covering the gazebo.

Were I not engaged in putting pen to paper,
I should unfurl my umbrella and walk
the freshened trail and photograph nature
shaking off its confinement, as I do mine.

Somewhere aloft, an osprey pierces the silence
With its clear, distinctive one-note call, a hawk
Competes with its clear calls of three that bring
Family from secret shelters farther into the woods.

Sparrows, again emboldened, twitter and flutter
from one green haven to another, happy to fly.
In truth, this place is not about my industry. The
pavilion is a sanctuary, my retreat from noise and
foolishness fostered by public manners gone begging.

Still, I must persist, assigning a series of words to
a system of understanding and resist the lure
that tantalizes. My wilting paper says that time
teeters between writing one more line and taking

leave from my sanctuary. Piqued, I pack, my thoughts
unfinished and restless, longing for my pen's productive
flow. Tomorrow. Tomorrow—another day in which
to marshal the pictures in my mind to words on paper.

About the Author

Shirley Foor began writing in the freelance market more than 50 years ago. Freelance writing allowed her to earn a little money while she stayed home with her four children.

Then Shirley's husband broke his back, and Shirley became the breadwinner. Her background in freelance writing gave her entry to a job as a features writer at the local newspaper in Moline, Il. Over the years, she was a reporter, chief of three bureau offices, and assistant regional editor.

When she was denied promotion to the Regional Editor's position because she was "unqualified," she left Illinois for a City Editor's job at a Knight-Ridder newspaper in Bradenton, FL, She was the first female city editor and later became the first female managing editor at that newspaper.

Shirley left journalism after 20 years and continued to write about her experiences and observations for family and friends, breaking from the "facts only" regimen of journalism to pursue the freedom and the joy of creative nonfiction storytelling. The facts are there, so is the context of the moment and the experience. This book is a collection of stories from the archives of Stories Foortold.

You can contact Shirley at:

Shirley J Foor
7322 Manatee Ave. W #122
Bradenton, FL. 34209-3441
foorwords@aol.com

www.ingramcontent.com/pod-product-compliance
Lightning Source LLC
Chambersburg PA
CBHW021931040426
42448CB00008B/1010